D1613515

CHAOS AND CONTEXT

CHAOS AND CONTEXT:

A Study in William James

by
Charlene Haddock Seigfried

OHIO UNIVERSITY PRESS
ATHENS, OHIO

Copyright © 1978 by Charlene Haddock Seigfried
ISBN 0-8214-0378-8
Printed in the United States of America by
Oberlin Printing Co., Inc.

Library of Congress Cataloging in Publication Data

Seigfried, Charlene Haddock, 1943–
    Chaos and context.

    Bibliography: p.
    Includes index.
    1. James, William, 1842–1910.   I.   Title.
B945.J24S44   150'.92'4   77-86346
ISBN 0-8244-0378-8

To Mom, Dad, Dick, Bob, John, Teri, Tom, and Jim,
because it's the first,
and to Hans and Karl Erik,
because it won't be the last.

TABLE OF CONTENTS

FOREWORD

THE THOUGHT of William James has long been identified with that controversial philosophical movement known as Pragmatism. This has turned out to be an unfortunate development, for although a pragmatic epistemology is an important strand in James's philosophy, it does not occupy the center of his vision. To the contrary, James's most important philosophical contention has to do with the status of relations and the philosophical implications of that contention, which he subsequently referred to as radical empiricism. Shortly after James's death, one of his most indefatigable and perceptive opponents, F. H. Bradley, wrote that "I can imagine no task more interesting to, and more incumbent on, the disciples of Professor James, than to make an attempt in earnest to explain and develop his doctrine of Radical Empiricism."

Yet, with the exception of the work of Ralph Barton Perry, James's student, colleague and intellectual biographer, little was done to further explicate and develop the meaning of radical empiricism, until the last decade when the thought of James was again considered in its entirety. The sources of this renewed interest in the philosophy of James are multiple. Some are due to those students of phenomenology, who were interested in James's influence on Husserl and in his work on consciousness. Further concern for James's philosophy was traceable to those who were working out a new language of personal sensibility, be it religious or moral and who found in James a novelty of perception and expression. Still others of us believed that James was an original philosopher of such importance that it became necessary to study him both historically and developmentally.

It is also important to recognize that James's influence on other thinkers is now known to be extensive, reaching to, among others, Husserl, Wittgenstein, Bergson, Royce, Dewey, Mead, Unamuno, Whitehead, Gertrude Stein and Niels Bohr. One upshot of this renewed interest in James's philosophy is that we are now clear about his central focus, which is unquestionably the status of relations. And that sets the stage for the importance of this book by Charlene Haddock Seigfried. It is the only full-length analysis of James's doctrine of relations and, as we shall see, it is exquisitely and originally presented. The considerable significance of this work by Professor Seigfried is better grasped if we know something of the textual disarray attendant on James's development of his position.

James first put forth his claim that relations are equally experienced as are the poles of those relations, in an essay entitled "On Some Omissions of Introspective Psychology," published in *Mind* in January of 1884. At that time, James wrote that "we ought to say a feeling of *and*, a feeling of *if*, a feeling of *but*, and a feeling of *by*, quite as readily as we say a feeling of *blue* or a feeling of *cold*." This text and other portions of the essay were repeated in the famous chapter on "The Stream of Thought," published in *The Principles of Psychology* (1890). Despite the dramatic claims of that chapter, relative to consciousness as a flow or a stream, the remainder of the *Principles* honored a functional dualism between physical object and mental state. Radical empiricism was simmering but had not yet been announced. In a "Preface" to *The Will To Believe and Other Essays in Popular Philosophy*, written in 1890, James proclaims that his philosophical "attitude" is one of "radical empiricism" which he describes somewhat elliptically in an attack on monism as a final philosophical position.

In the next half-decade, James was occupied with other concerns, especially with the problems and materials which were to culminate in his classic work on *The Varieties of Religious Experience* (1902). Nonetheless, in his teaching at Harvard and in the raft of Notebooks he compiled, James returned again and again to the nagging problem of the status of relations and his still gestating doctrine of radical empiricism. In 1904, he wrote a letter to François Pillon in which he described his philosophical position. "My philosophy is what I call a radical empiricism, a pluralism, a 'tychism,' which represents order as being gradually won and always in the making. . . . I am sure that, be it in the end judged true or false, it is essential to the evolution of clearness in philosophic thought that *someone* should defend a pluralistic empiricism radically."

James then set out to do just that. During the years 1904 and 1905, James wrote essays on those problems he ascertained as central to radical empiricism. He especially focused on the meaning of consciousness, the activity of cognition and, above all, on the status of relations. It is also at this time that James proposed his controversial postulate of pure experience, now given careful scrutiny in the present book by Professor Seigfried. James intended to publish these essays in a volume and in 1907 recorded a tentative table of contents on the outside of a manila folder which contained reprints of the essays. Shortly thereafter *Pragmatism* was published and James was drawn into a polemical response. When he published *The Meaning of Truth* in 1909, he used some of the essays from the projected radical empiricism book. Still other essays from that intended collection found their way into *A Pluralistic Universe*. The result of these decisions was the destruction of a coherent book devoted to radical empiricism.

We know that James did not abandon his commitment to radical empiricism, for it is in the "Preface" to *The Meaning of Truth* that he offers his most explicit statement of its meaning. Twenty-five years after his first claim about the status of relations, in the aforementioned essay of 1884, "On Some Omissions of Introspective Psychology," James now repeats the claim, in slightly changed but stronger language. "The statement of fact is that the relations between things, conjunctive as well as disjunctive, are just as much matters of direct particular experience, neither more so nor less so, than the things themselves."

The full significance of this "statement of fact" by James was difficult to assess, for the essays intended originally to sustain it were now scattered in different volumes, devoted to other interests. In 1912, two years after the death of James, Ralph Barton Perry collected a group of essays written by James and published them under the title of *Essays in Radical Empiricism*. This book differed from James's original intentions, especially in that it left out several early essays, among them "The Function of Cognition" (1885) and "The Knowing of Things Together" (1895). Consequently, despite the fact that Perry's edition had a coherence and an intrinsic interest of its own, James's radical empiricism was severed from the earlier psychological and philosophical foundations which he had so carefully nurtured. Further, after James's death, pragmatism dominated the philosophical climate, and James's thought was dragged, posthumously, into a fray which did not represent the center of his vision. Coming full circle, I repeat my earlier remark that only recently has James's philosophy been studied in a way which is cognizant of its rich and varied themes. And this, in turn, leads me to an assessment of the book in hand by Professor Seigfried.

As a student of the philosophy of William James for the past twenty-five years, I have long felt the need for a detailed and systematic analysis of the development of his doctrine of relations. That is exactly what Professor Seigfried has accomplished. Better yet, she has written this impressive book with technical skill and with clarity of style. When one considers the complexity of the issues, it is astonishing how economical and compressed is her exposition. Her prose is not bloated or distracted but keeps a focus throughout the text. And she is particularly able at conjoining exposition and argument.

Professor Seigfried approaches James's doctrine of relations from three vantage points. In my judgment, this decision is correct. First, she accounts for the development of James's position, starting with his *Psychology* and continuing on through the *Essays in Radical Empiricism*. Second, she presents and evaluates the doctrine itself and in so doing, confronts the thorny issue of the postulate of pure experience. The title of her book, *Chaos and Context*, points to an original interpretation of "pure experience," and her explanatory chapter is the most helpful that I have read on that subject. Third, she has James, once again, confront his opponents. Here she isolates Hume and Bradley as representative figures of the two alternative positions which James long worried over. Her presentation in those chapters is lucid, integral and serves to highlight both the difficulties and originality of James's formulation. Each of these three vantage points is essential for any comprehensive understanding of James's doctrine of relations. The version of them given by Professor Seigfried will take its place in the canon of James studies as indispensable to those seeking an ordered and coherent exposition of his position.

Although Professor Seigfried does not allow her own predilections to interrupt the flow of her philosophical narrative, she does leave us with an intriguing last chapter on "The Malleability of Experience." Her appellation for "pure experience" as a "quasi-chaos" leads her to some imaginative reflection on the constructive activity of conceptualization. In short, she reads James's other consuming interest, that of the organism as natively selective, back into the postulate of pure experience. This strikes me as a sound approach, not only in terms of James's philosophy but as a point of departure for subsequent philosophical speculation on the nature of human activity. If experience is as malleable as James and Seigfried contend, then the task is to diagnose and evaluate the ways by which we impose ourselves and so construct a world, our world. The "Conclusion" to her book is actually an appeal to take up such a project in the context of James's claim about relations.

In William James's private papers at Harvard University, one finds a Notebook numbered N^{vii}, which is filled with reflections on radical empiricism. On the outside cover, James cited his friend Benjamin Blood by writing, "The writhing serpent of philosophy is one gigantic string of mare's nests." Although no mere mortal will unravel that string, *Chaos and Context* by Charlene Haddock Seigfried is a distinctive and creative accomplishment which continues and enhances the life-long effort of William James to understand the meaning of relations.

John J. McDermott
Queens College, C.U.N.Y.

PREFACE

BEFORE I BEGAN WORK on William James's philosophy I surveyed the field of secondary literature, and not finding much that threw light on the specific aspect I was taking up, the status of relations in radical empiricism, concentrated instead on the texts themselves. Some time after the completion of the manuscript I had occasion to compile a William James bibliography and in so doing discovered some interesting literature written in the interim. Some of the more trenchant insights have been alluded to, either by incorporating a reference to them in the body of the work or, more often, in the notes. There was no need, however, to alter the original interpretation of James's position as given in his published works.

The Harvard series of The Works of William James, with their definitive texts and extensive critical apparatus, will no doubt become the standard reference books cited in James studies. I have, therefore, used their pagination for the books in print so far, which are, at this time, *Pragmatism, The Meaning of Truth, Essays in Radical Empiricism,* and *A Pluralistic Universe.*

I would like to thank Professors Robert Barry and John J. McDermott for carefully reading the manuscript and enthusiastically encouraging me to publish it. I especially appreciate Professor McDermott's generosity in writing the Foreword. He has a detailed introduction to the *Essays in Radical Empiricism,* in the Harvard series mentioned above, which is an indispensable adjunct to understanding them. Professor Hans Seigfried, who still hasn't read the manuscript in its entirety, nonetheless was always willing and eager to discuss the many issues I was puzzling over and to offer constructive criticism. Lastly, I would like to thank my son, Karl Erik, whose imminent appearance encouraged me to finish working in good time.

Evanston, Illinois, April, 1977

KEY TO ABBREVIATIONS

The original publication data are given in the Bibliography,
part I

WILLIAM JAMES

Principles—The Principles of Psychology. I and II., New York: Dover
Publications, 1950.

W.B.—The Will to Believe and Other Essays in Popular Philosophy.
New York: Dover Publications, 1956.

Prag.—Pragmatism. The Works of William James. Ed. by Fredson
Bowers and Ignas K. Skrupskelis. Cambridge: Harvard University Press, 1975.

M.T.—The Meaning of Truth. The Works of William James. Ed. by
Fredson Bowers and Ignas K. Skrupskelis. Cambridge: Harvard
University Press, 1975.

P.U.—A Pluralistic Universe. The Works of William James. Ed. by
Frederick H. Burkhardt. Cambridge: Harvard University Press,
1977.

S.P.P.—Some Problems of Philosophy. New York: Longmans, Green,
and Co., 1911.

E.R.E.—Essays in Radical Empiricism. The Works of William James.
Ed. by Fredson Bowers and Ignas K. Skrupskelis. Cambridge:
Harvard University Press, 1976.

DAVID HUME

Treatise.—A Treatise of Human Nature. Ed. by L. A. Selby-Bigge.
Oxford: Clarendon Press, 1967.

*Enquiry.—Hume's Enquiries Concerning the Human Understanding
and Concerning the Principles of Morals.* Ed. by L. A. Selby-
Bigge. Oxford: Clarendon Press, 1902.

INTRODUCTION

THE OBVIOUS continuity of experience poses no problems for the un-reflecting person; indeed, the fluidity of experience is not even ad-verted to. But once reflection and discrimination begin, with the distinction of subject and object, thinker and thing, then the various relationships of subject to object, of objects within the physical world among themselves, and of mental processes among themselves, become problematic. Even on the purely descriptive level, it makes a difference whether I say, " 'A' is next to 'B' " or "I see that 'A' is next to 'B'," but it is only when these different descriptions are analyzed and justified that the status of relations becomes an object of inquiry and debate. According to James, that philosophy is most successful which can 'ground' conceptualized relationships in the immediacy of experience. The success of his own philosophic enterprise stands or falls ac-cording to whether his doctrine of radical empiricism can demonstrate that "immediately experienced conjunctive relations are as real as anything else."[1] The credibility of his insights depends to a large ex-tent on his success in clarifying the constitution of relations in such a way as to neutralize the all too obvious contradictions which arise from his asserting in his various works both chaos and order, i.e., both a structured and an unstructured paradigm experience. Even if James did not explicitly resolve the contradiction himself, he will still have made a significant contribution to the theory of relations if a coherent case can be made for an explanation which will coordinate and eluci-date some of his most philosophically promising insights.

Radical empiricism is the name James gave to his entire philosophy, but he sums up its major points in the preface to *The Meaning of Truth*, where he defines radical empiricism as consisting of a postu-late, a statement of fact, and a generalized conclusion.

The postulate is that the only things that shall be debatable among philosophers shall be things definable in terms drawn from experience. . . .

The statement of fact is that the relations between things, conjunctive as well as disjunctive, are just as much matters of direct particular experience, neither more so nor less so, than the things themselves.

The generalized conclusion is that therefore the parts of experience hold together from next to next by relations that are themselves parts of experience. The directly apprehended universe needs, in short, no extraneous trans-empirical connective support, but possesses in its own right a concatenated or continuous structure.[2]

In *The Will to Believe*, written twelve years earlier (1897), he gives a less technical explanation of his central insight, emphasizing somewhat different aspects. He calls his philosophy "empirical" in order to emphasize the hypothetical character of all conclusions concerning matters of fact, since any conclusion may be altered in the course of future experience. The epithet "radical" is meant to indicate that "the world is a pluralism; as we find it, its unity seems to be that of any collection."[3] This pluralism consists of two assertions, one is "the opacity of the finite facts as merely given," and the other is the importance of points of view in philosophizing about the world (*W.B.*, vii).

It would seem contradictory to claim the "givenness" of "mere facts" while emphasizing the importance of one's point of view in discerning what is fact and what is fiction, but James sees them as interdependent in that what is explainable from one point of view is a bare datum or "externality" from another. James argues that all points of view are limited, since there is for us no absolute perspective outside of our experienced world from which the world would appear as unified in its totality. Whether there is an absolute point of view for an "Absolute" is outside the realm of philosophical discourse. The limitedness of points of view means that there will always be mere facts unexplainable from any particular point of view, which can only be accepted as given. However, since what is a mere datum from one point of view may be accounted for systematically from another point of view, it would seem to follow that ultimately every datum would be context-dependent when and if enough points of view could be correlated. This sounds very close to Peirce's community of investigators. Although this conclusion cannot be ruled out in principle, since pluralism, if it is to remain empiricist, must be a hypothetical postulate, not a dogmatic assertion, it is highly unlikely. A community of investigators would represent but one more point of view. Even the totality of finite investigators would be a finite number, which could not represent every possible point of view. The community of investiga-

2

tors as a limit concept would be foreign to James, who speaks in terms of the individual, but as a concept, he would class it with the concept of an absolute point of view, that is, as outside of all experience and therefore philosophically questionable.

Although James argues for distinct points of view, his philosophy is not solipsistic, and even though in his description of things he "starts with the parts and makes of the whole a being of the second order," he emphasizes continuity (*E.R.E.*, 22). What holds together distinct points of view and a shared world as well as individual data and conceptualization of them is his "statement of fact" concerning the reality of relations. In *Essays in Radical Empiricism*, James's most 'technical' explanation of his philosophy, he argues that "the relations that connect experiences must themselves be experienced relations, and any kind of relation experienced must be accounted as 'real' as anything else in the system" (*E.R.E.*, 22). I intend to scrutinize James's theory of relations in order to see if it can bear the weight of his philosophy. More specifically, to elaborate the doctrine of pure experience as an insight that, by dismantling all forms of dualism at one blow, opens the way for the solution of otherwise unresolvable problems. The chaos-order distinction, like the subject-object, knower-known, and percept-concept distinctions, will be seen to be second order realities which can be more fruitfully handled from a perspective of the first order reality of pure experience. The difficult problem of the status of pure experience will be analyzed as well as the relation of pure to 'impure' or ordinary experience. The still puzzling difficulty of how determined given relations are, with the concomitant problem of unchangeable versus malleable relations will be explored. Since without the doctrine of experienced relations the doctrine of pure experience would be vacuous, it is imperative to see how the theory of relations holds up under scrutiny.

C. I. Lewis, in "A Pragmatic Conception of the A Priori," formulates what is perhaps the most damaging criticism of the pragmatic program: "Pragmatism has sometimes been charged with oscillating between two contrary notions; the one, that experience is 'through and through malleable to our purpose,' the other, that facts are 'hard' and uncreated by the mind."[4] A completely indeterminate experience which can be shaped at will with no regard to established facts would negate the shared world presupposed in all knowledge claims, while experience as consisting exclusively of hard facts, independent of the human context from which they derive their meaning, would ignore the primacy of the subject in shaping experiences. In order to state the problem more clearly, I would like to characterize experience,

3

facts, and established facts. Since experience, for James, is the primal reality prior to all distinctions, whether metaphysical or epistemological, it cannot be described in the usual dualistic terms as the subject's contribution in relation to that which is given.[5] Let it suffice at this point to give a sketchy indication of what experience is, rather than a strict definition, the very preciseness of which would be a distortion. By 'experience' I mean, minimally, a certain emphasis within the flux of temporal processes. By 'facts' I mean, as Professor Hanson does, the "*structural* possibilities inherent within states of affairs such that some statements made about these states will be certifiably true and some will be certifiably false," and by 'established facts' I mean the formulations of such structural possibilities and their acceptance by a given community.[6]

The pragmatic position may have vacillated between the two interpretations of experience, as either malleable or as already structured, because of the difficulties inherent in accepting either position as adequate by itself. If experience is described as completely indeterminate and arbitrary, then it can have no necessary connection to established facts. Therefore, experience as completely indeterminate or subjective could not serve as the basis of an objective understanding of the world, since it would have no common characteristics. On the other hand, if experience is described as completely objective, i.e., that everyone experiences the world in the same way (or that all perceptions of the same are the same), then one cannot account for the world as changing and subject to divergent interpretations. Although neither position makes sense in isolation, they cannot be joined without contradiction. If pragmatism has avoided the confrontation of these opposing views by eclectically borrowing from both, then it would be flawed in its basic assumptions.

This would be especially true for James, since he characterized his own position as that of radical empiricism, which is based on the postulate that the only things "debatable among philosophers shall be things definable in terms drawn from experience" (*M.T.*, 6). If his explanation of experience involves a fundamental contradiction, then his philosophic program is vitiated from the outset. That this might be the case is intimated by John J. McDermott in his introduction to *The Writings of William James*, where he says that "in effect, James appeals to direct experience but seems reluctant to let go of some of the large organizing categories, which in other philosophical contexts are seen as *a priori*."[7] Furthermore, John E. Smith does not think that James ever resolved this problem. McDermott thinks that the question is still open "whether it can be resolved as an extension of James's radically empirical point of view."[8] I propose to show that James's seminal idea of experience can be explained coherently and without contradiction by extending and refining his own principles through exhibiting the interconnection of his postulates about experience with his theory of relations.

According to James's radical empiricism, experience can be explicated only in conjunction with a statement of fact, *viz.*, that "relations between things, conjunctive as well as disjunctive, are just as much matters of direct particular experience, neither more so nor less so, than the things themselves" (*M.T.*, 7).[9] Radical empiricism depends heavily on the reality of relations, and it is the working out of this position that distinguishes this philosophical movement from idealism on the one hand and empiricism on the other. Consequently, the problem of whether a consistent and non-trivial theory of experience can be maintained within James's philosophy of radical empiricism can be resolved only by a careful elucidation and application of his theory of relations. Although John E. Smith concurs with James's theory that conjunctive relations are really found in experience and not imposed on it, he does not think that all relations can be developed from pure experience, but some must be classed as *a priori* in that they involve a synthetic or constructive activity on the part of the one who knows.[10] He argues that a doctrine of a world of pure experience consistently adhered to would lead to an unreasonable world since "the stream of experience is neither self-organizing nor self-interpreting."[11]

I think that this latter formulation encapsulates a basic misunderstanding which would prevent us from recognizing the significance of an important aspect of James's theory of relations. To clear up this misunderstanding, though, a careful consideration of James's theory of pure experience, which Smith also pointed out as one of the two basic claims of radical empiricism, must be tempered by a regard for consistency not always shared by James. The stream of experience cannot ultimately be reduced to interpreter and interpreted or organizer and organized, since, in its immediacy, experience is not dualistically composed of thought and thing; these are later additions that can themselves be reduced to, or seen to arise out of, an originally undifferentiated process.

This study will begin with an explication of James's psychological doctrines of the stream of consciousness and empirically sensed relations in order to demonstrate their continuity with his later theory of pure experience. At the same time, a significant discontinuity will also become apparent as the key to the transformation from a psychological to a philosophical perspective, namely, his abandonment of the

5

dualism of his earlier view and his realization of the pluralistic value
of a doctrine of pure experience in illuminating the structure of ordinary
experience. The larger part of the study will seek to demonstrate that
the thesis of pure experience as developed in James's later writings can
be maintained only if it can be shown that relations are really given
in experience, and yet need the specification of a context to differen-
tiate them. Although James himself lapses into inconsistency, sometimes affirming the reality of intrinsic relations and sometimes claim-
ing that relations are extrinsically imposed, such contradictions can be
avoided by joining James's thesis of immediately experienced conjunctive relations in sensation, actual in their immediacy but not in their
specific construction, with his realization of the context-dependency of
all relations which have been explicitly grasped in their intellectual-
ized form. This solution to the problem of 'given' versus 'constructed'
relations depends on the distinction between pure, undifferentiated experience and experience as entering into particular, articulated contexts.

James, like Kant, attempted to utilize the insights of the empiricists
and the rationalists, and both began by accepting Hume's challenge
as to the givenness of relations in experience. Unlike Kant, James
did not approach the problem systematically nor did he rely on the
conceptual tools which rationalism had forged. As a result, James's
solutions were not accorded the attention and controversy in philosophical circles which Kant's system received. It was understood that James
had somehow managed to come out on the other side of the empiricist-
rationalist controversy, but in a rather haphazard way, and thus his
many trenchant insights were only elaborated and applied one by one
as they happened to strike the reader or listener. James's continuous attempt to overcome the classic dualism inherent in both the empirical and
rational traditions has recently been accorded the attention it deserves
as one of the roots of the controversy over the pragmatic conception
of the *a priori*. Unfortunately, the inconsistencies of James's exposition
have resulted all too often in the attention span extending only long
enough to dismiss his solution as unworkable. This study seeks to
give a more sustained presentation of James's position, trying to rem-
edy its defects and letting its assets appear in an orderly way. James's
'dialogues' with Hume and Bradley will be critically examined, as they
expose the uniqueness of James's position in relation to the two main
philosophical alternatives available in opposition to his own: empiricism
and rationalism.

Although chronology plays a part in determining James's mature
position, much more important is style and redundancy. Most of his
works were originally given as lectures and consequently employ a

6

popular mode of exposition, an imprecise vocabulary, and frequent exaggeration for the sake of effect. As Perry comments, "James has something of the quality of a pamphleteer. After the *Principles*, all of his works were either lectures or special articles, written with a view to their immediate effect upon an audience or philosophical opponent."[12] There are some exceptions to this "squashy popular-lecture style"; they are the posthumously published *Essays in Radical Empiricism*, written originally as articles for philosophical periodicals, to be read by scholars, also some replies to critics in *The Meaning of Truth*, and some portions of *Some Problems of Philosophy*.[13] The most important work, both from the point of view of philosophy and of the theory of relations, is the *Essays in Radical Empiricism*, from which I have drawn the most extended analysis. His other works have been brought in insofar as they illuminate various aspects presented there. *The Principles of Psychology* also occupies a unique place among James's works: it is his most sustained scholarly endeavor and contains the seeds of much of his later speculation. For these reasons it has also been given special attention.[14] Redundancy is also more important than chronology in a study of James: James used over and over again those insights which he considered most important and illuminating, often lifting whole passages and chapters from book to book. An example of such repetition is chapter six of *Essays in Radical Empiricism*, "The Experience of Activity," which is introduced by this footnote:

> President's Address before the American Psychological Association, Philadelphia Meeting, December, 1904. Reprinted from *The Psychological Review*, vol. Xii, No. 1, Jan., 1905. Also reprinted, with some omissions, as Appendix B, *A Pluralistic Universe*, pp. 370-394. Pp. 166-167 have also been reprinted in *Some Problems of Philosophy*, p. 212.[15]

Thus, the importance of particular aspects of James's thought can be roughly determined by how often he repeated them, and whether he still included them in his later works. A study of these later works recapitulates the most important aspects of his earlier ones, making extensive cross-referencing of the same topic unnecessary.

James wrote thematically rather than systematically or logically. As a result, his "meanderings, zigzags, and circles" affected people as "incidental remarks of great merit," which profoundly influenced both technical philosophers and men of arts and letters in every field.[16] James himself encouraged such a piecemeal approach to his work, often by bragging of its purposeful non-technical approach. In a letter of May 18, 1907, he writes, "All that humanism needs now is to make *applications* of itself to special problems. Get a school of youngsters at work. Refutations of error should be left to the rationalist alone. They are a stock function of that school."[17] There is a less well known side of James, though, which comes through in some of his letters:

> I am interested in a metaphysical system ('Radical Empiricism') which has been forming itself within me, more interested, in fact, than I have ever been in anything else; but it is very difficult to get it into shape for any connected exposition: and though it contains very practical elements, I find it almost impossible to put it into popular form.[18]

> I actually *hate* lecturing; and this job condemns me to publish another book written in picturesque and popular style when I was settling down to something whose manner would be more *strengwissenschaftlich*, i.e., concise, dry, and impersonal.[19]

James was convinced of the barrenness of much philosophical speculation, but he also valued the precision of conceptualization insofar as it provided a shortcut to a more human appropriation of experience. Especially in his mature years, he longed to write a sustained and coherent exposition of his philosophy and answer his critics in an irrefutable way. In the letter to Schiller of May 18, 1907, already quoted, James chides Schiller for rebutting Bradley's absolutism in a long and complex polemical article, but James himself had been writing article after article, letter after letter, in an identical attempt.[20]

It is no disservice, then, to James to present various aspects of his thought in a more tightly knit philosophical mode. There is more to James than "incidental remarks," and if his writings do not give evidence of a careful systematic approach, his letters and unpublished notes give many hints and outlines of such a project. It would, nevertheless, still be a mutilation of James's philosophy to distill it, without remainder, into a few isolated propositions and consequences. In this study I have followed as closely as possible James's own thematic approach, drawing together various aspects under a unified topic and following up the related themes which present themselves in the course of elucidation. Although this untangling of knots of interrelated themes allows many loose ends to unravel, it is hoped that they are intertwined again in later chapters and in the conclusion. In order to approach a coherent presentation of James's theory of relations, it has been necessary, after exposing some undeniable contradictions which emerge from a survey of James's entire opus, to select those proposals of his which allow for the most coherent over-all explanation. In other words, I have attempted to reconstruct a consistent theory of the status of relations in the spirit, and as close to the letter as possible, of William James.

CHAPTER ONE

PHILOSOPHICAL THEMES IN
THE PRINCIPLES OF PSYCHOLOGY

THE CONSTITUTION OF OBJECTS AND RELATIONS

ALTHOUGH, in the jargon of the day, James sided with the empiricists against the rationalists, he disavowed the simple impressions of Locke and Hume. He held that, contrary to their claims, persons are not conscious of one sensation and then another, but of a teeming multiplicity of objects and relations.[1] Simple sensations, far from being primary data or building blocks out of which more complicated objects are constructed, are rather the result of a discriminative attention which isolates single elements out of myriad concatenations of variously organized sensations. In this early explanation of consciousness James does not seem to have the problem of the constitution of objects and relations because for him consciousness means consciousness of already constituted objects and relations, and the elements of the constitutions can only be discriminated in a second act of consciousness, that is, they belong to a secondary order of explanation rather than the primary order of simple consciousness. However, since consciousness is not of single objects and relations but of a "teeming multiplicity of objects and relations" the problem of their constitution still has to be raised. How do we get *an* object and *a* relation from myriad objects and relations? In what sense can we be said to be conscious of objects and relations at all in the immediacy of consciousness before we are aware of a single object or relation? What, exactly, is James opposing to the simple sensations of the British empiricists? In this chapter an attempt will be made to organize answers to these questions to the extent that James treats of them in *The Principles of Psychology*. In doing so it will become apparent that James is less interested in the constitution of objects and relations as such than in emphasizing the multiplicity of objects and relations—the richness (or chaos) of experience far beyond any attempts to organize it—as against the seemingly rigorous derivation of simple ideas from simple impressions.

Although at this time James was not yet in full possession of the insight that consciousness is not an entity, he carefully avoided setting up a person-consciousness dichotomy.[2] Not being able, in good English, to say "it thinks," he preferred to speak of "thought going on" as presupposing the least assumptions about the nature of thought. In brief, the five characteristics of thought which will be further elaborated in pursuing the particular problematic of this chapter are:

1) Every thought tends to be part of a personal consciousness.
2) Within each personal consciousness thought is always changing.
3) Within each personal consciousness thought is sensibly continuous.
4) It always appears to deal with objects independent of itself.
5) It is interested in some parts of these objects to the exclusion of others, and welcomes or rejects—*chooses* from among them, in a word —all the while. (225)

Consciousness appears to itself as a continuous process, a stream of thought. In a striking metaphor James compares this flow of thought to the rhythm of a bird in its flights and perchings. Just as the flight of a bird is punctuated with brief respites, the flow of thought is punctuated by "resting-places." These "perchings" are particular sensorial imaginations which arrest the flow to the extent that certain combinations of sense impressions can be isolated, contemplated, and remembered. Connecting and flowing around these fixed sensory units are thoughts of relations. "Let us call the resting-places the 'substantive parts,' and the places of flight the 'transitive parts,' of the stream of thought" (243). By using this metaphor of the rhythm of a bird James tries to evoke in his audience their own experience of consciousness and direct their attention to certain aspects of it. At this introductory level a conceptual description alone would not work as well as the metaphor to stimulate an experience of consciousness which can then serve as a reference point for a more elaborate explanation.

A fundamental thesis of James is that once it is granted that feelings exist and that real relations also exist in nature, then it must be

11

granted that those relations are mirrored or known by feelings (245).[3] Feelings of relations exist just as surely as do the relations in nature which are experienced. James is well aware of the philosophical doctrines which either deny that relations exist outside of the mind, or that we have any perceptions of such relations if they do exist.[4] His arguments for the reality of relations *extra mentum* and for a con-comitant perception of them reappear in various forms throughout his writings since he considered these assertions as underpinning his psychological and later, philosophical, position. The argument put forward at this point is that human speech reflects a firm belief in various relations between objects of thought through syntactic form, conjunctions, prepositions, and adverbial phrases, as well as in voice inflection.[5] All of these aspects of speech exhibit various shades of relations. If the argument stopped at this point, with a mere appeal to ordinary usage, without an effort to go beyond unexamined and uncritically accepted speech usage, then nothing much could be concluded from such an appeal, since almost any sort of nonsense can be derived from a literal recital of the quirks of ordinary language. Furthermore, those philosophers who deny that relations can be ex-perienced do not thereby deny that language and speech express innumerable relations, but question whether this usage reflects some-thing rationally tenable.

In assessing the importance of the relations exhibited in both the structure and speech of language James makes the claim that "if we speak objectively, it is the real relations that appear revealed; if we speak subjectively, it is the stream of consciousness that matches each of them by an inward coloring of its own" (245). James not only appeals to the structure of language to support his contention that experienced relations are embedded in the form and inflection of language, but he also criticizes the narrowness of the use of feeling or perception words in regard to their object. Besides speaking of a feeling of 'blue' and a feeling of 'cold', we should also speak of a feeling of 'if' and of 'by' and of 'but'. The basis for the assertion that we ought to speak of feelings of relations according to the same pattern of speech that we speak of feelings of 'hot' or 'hard' is that we experience both sorts of feelings just as directly. It may seem strange to say that we feel 'next to' in the same way that we feel 'bright' but we do experience both just as immediately, as in the single perception of something bright next to something dull. We do not see something bright and then in a second act of seeing perceive something dull and then in an act of reflection conclude that the bright thing is next to the dull thing. Rather we see "brightthingnexttodullthing" in one glance and only later discriminate out the elements. It is entirely arbitrary to class 'next to' as being of a different order than 'bright thing'. Both are equally given. To see 'brightthing' as a-bright-thing requires as much discriminatory attention as to see that 'brightthing' is *next to* 'dullthing'.

James concedes that although we ought to say that we have a feeling of 'by' just as we say that we have a feeling of 'blue', we actually do not. He ascribes this peculiarity to the fact that language does not lend itself to such usage because it has been habitually used to express only substantive parts as objects of feelings. Consequently it does not lend itself to expressing the transitive aspect of experience as the object of feelings. In other words, it sounds queer to say: "I saw 'and'," but not queer to say: "I saw 'blue'," even though the sentence, "I saw a blue ball and a yellow ball," is perfectly normal and may express a single impression of blue-ball-along-with-yellow-ball. To say that language refuses to lend itself to any other use than that of expressing the substantive parts of our feelings because of our habit of recognizing the existence of the substantive parts alone, only moves the argument back one step. It must still be asked why it is that we only recognize the substantive parts of the stream of consciousness. By this James cannot mean that we only experience the substantive parts because he has already said that we are conscious of both the substantive and the transitive aspects of consciousness. What he must mean is that although we experience both, we only pay attention to, or focus on, ("perch on") the substantive parts. James does not at this point go into the reason why we only recognize the existence of the substantive parts, but further on in the volume indicates that it is due to the selectivity of the mind (284 ff.).

Language can be misleading in many ways. Empiricists have already pointed out the philosophical tendency to people the world with myriads of abstract entities and forces merely because names exist which name them, as though the mere existence of a name were sufficient proof for the separate existence of that which is named.[6] The opposite error is equally unacceptable to James. He denies the assumption that where no name exists no entity can exist. In fact James tends to over-populate rather than under-populate the world. "Namelessness is compatible with existence" because consciousness (and later, experience), not language, is the final court of appeal (251). James gives as an example of nameless existences, which we nevertheless experience, the innumerable consciousnesses of emptiness, no one of which is exactly like another, and yet no nomenclature exists to set one off from another. Language, not consciousness, is found

13

wanting. Rather than saying that relations do not exist in reality because they do not appear as objects in ordinary sentence structure, it would be more accurate to say that the innumerable relations and their subtle distinctions in the stream of consciousness cannot be adequately expressed in any language.[7]

James does not want to start with a unified theory of consciousness, with all terms precisely delineated, because then only those aspects of consciousness can be caught in the theoretical net which are large enough and conformable to a clearly articulated configuration. Since much more flows through and around such a conceptual net than is caught, James prefers to "dive into the stream" and explain what is there. He does this in this instance by reasserting the vague as a descriptive category to be considered when treating consciousness.[8] "The ridiculous theory of Hume and Berkeley that we can have no images but of perfectly definite things" is rejected as is the notion that only simple objective qualities are subjectively apprehended and not objective relations (254–5). Consciousness as a stream or process of substantive and transitive rhythms is preferred as a descriptive model to that of single impressions producing single ideas, as though strung out on a string, one after another.

When considering the cognitive function of different states of mind, James finds that he can divide knowledge into the two broad categories, distinguishable in practice, of knowledge of acquaintance and knowledge-about. He had earlier characterized the former as knowledge immediately obtained and thus recognized but without the ability to be communicated to others, who must themselves become acquainted with whatever is known in this way. Included in this incommunicable way of mere acquaintance are "all the elementary natures of the world, its highest genera, the simple qualities of matter and mind, together with the kinds of relation that subsist between them" (221). Knowledge-about, on the other hand, can be described and communicated, its various relations articulated, and different mental operations performed upon it. Since in those able to speak at all, some communication of knowledge always enters in, this distinction is not an absolute but a relative one, and indicates the preponderance of one type of knowledge or the other. The less we analyze a thing, the more our familiarity with it can be classified as mere acquaintance. This explanation of two types of knowledge clarifies what James means by 'thought' and 'feeling', with thought including conceptions and judgments and with feeling including the emotions and sensations (222). In this case the reinstatement of the vague to its proper place is reinforced by the realization that knowledge-about and knowledge by acquaintance "is reducible almost entirely to the absence or presence of psychic fringes or overtones" (259).

Knowledge about a thing means a conceptual grasp of its relations, whereas acquaintance with it is limited to a bare impression of the thing while being vaguely aware of a 'fringe' of unarticulated affinities.[9] In all voluntary thinking there is some topic, vague mood, or goal which organizes or gives direction to that thinking. Out of all the images and phrases that are present to the consciousness, certain ones are picked out rather than others insofar as they are felt to be related to the topic or goal. The relations are more often felt than cognized, and only some are directly adverted to. The others remain on the fringe of consciousness, as it were. The most important aspect of relations felt on the fringe is the relation of harmony or discord they impart to the topic of thought. Those representations which are felt to further the topic are related harmoniously to it and the thought goes forward, those which do not, create a dissonance which is not resolved until the thought is furthered or completed.

In order to get from the vaguely intuited relation of the fringe to the center of focus, a further principle of selectivity must be introduced. The primordial chaos of sensations provides no basis for organizing an individual consciousness, rather, selectivity and attention constitute consciousness (288). Only what we agree to attend to shapes our mind: "without selective interest, experience is an utter chaos" (402). "We actually *ignore* most of the things before us" (284). Things are not independent entities which we must notice when brought within our purview, but are special groups of sensible qualities which interest us in some way and which we therefore substantialize and onto which we project a stable, independent existence. The mind selects, for practical or esthetic reasons, certain sensations as belonging properly to a thing. Some of the sensations are further selected as being essential to that thing, while others are considered to be mere appearances, modifiable without destroying the essence of that thing. In both cases the mind selects these attributes for reasons of its own, and not from any external compulsion.

The distinction being made is that between essence and accident or primary and secondary qualities. Some examples of selective interest determining which sensations are essential and which are mere appearances are as follows. In the case of concrete buildings seen on a sunny day and at sunset, we will consider the color of the building to be 'really' white, as it is in the day, and only 'appearing' to be rose-colored at sunset—even though we equally sense both. One is no more or less an appearance than the other, but we make the distinction. Sounds are

15

considered loud or quiet according to some optimal conditions, and distorted from this 'essential' sound by adverse conditions, e.g., a normally loud tone will appear quiet when heard from a distance. Although we sense the tone both times, we consider the first as essentially or really the tone under consideration, and the second as a mere appearance due to the distortion of distance.

The essential characteristics of a thing, which constitute its objectivity, are as much sensations selected out as are the so-called subjective conditions (286). Even the rational connections which the mind can adduce as substantiating its claims to objectivity are themselves the product of the selective activity of the mind itself, and are not due to any intrinsic property of the object. The selective power of the mind thus far explained sounds rather arbitrary, as though any sensation could be chosen to constitute any object, and any sensations, no matter how obtrusive, could be ignored. James neither affirms or denies absolute arbitrariness at this point, nor does he give any internal criteria for selection, even though external criteria seem *prima facie* ruled out. He does claim that the human race as a whole largely agrees on what it shall notice and name and what it shall ignore, but no evidence is brought forward in support of this claim (beyond the seminal hint that the whole universe is split into two halves comprising 'me' and 'not-me' nor any reason suggested as to why the human race should be so alike in its tastes. He does seem to give priority to the ethical interest in determining what to ignore and what to choose among many possible interests. The choice would become one of character primarily, and on the basis of what we would want to become, we would choose those interests most compatible with that character (288).

In clarifying one aspect of a thing as essential to it, rather than another, which would seem more essential under different circumstances, we are always unjust, partial, and exclusive (II, 333). The reason given for this partiality is no less than necessity, the necessity arising from our finite and practical nature. "My thinking is first and last and always for the sake of my doing, and I can only do one thing at a time" (II, 333). Things only interest us piecemeal, one or another aspect is important for the moment; we can be engaged in doing things only serially. Although the essence of paper may be its suitability as a writing surface when I am about to write a letter, its essence is its combustibility when I need it for starting a fire. Its characteristic as a writing surface is in no way essential to its usefulness or meaning as a fire-starter. The essence of a thing—that without which a thing would not be what it is—is determined for James according to the use we make of it. When classifying fire-starting materials, such as paper, kerosene, and sawdust, what essentially characterizes all of them is their combustibility. That the kerosene is transparent, the sawdust brown, and the paper suitable for writing on has no bearing on their essence as fire-starters. Any of these properties could change (the kerosene could become opaque with cinders, the sawdust could as well be red-colored, and the paper could be dipped in oil and thus made impermeable to ink) and the things in question would still remain what they are: combustible. The reality of objects overflows any of our narrow essential definitions of them. In fact, what we consider to be the essential characteristics of a thing characterizes us more than they characterize the thing (II, 334).

One consequence of the flow of thought in the stream of consciousness and of the seemingly unending number of sensations present to consciousness is that it cannot be assumed that we ever perceive the same sensation twice. We do, however, think that we grasp the same object (231). We habitually ignore the subjective aspect of sensations, using them merely to delineate realities whose presence they reveal. Since our sensibilities are changing all the time, the same object cannot easily be given to the same subject. Likewise, "for an identical sensation to recur it would have to occur the second time *in an unmodified brain,*" which is patently not the case (233). Even if an identical sensation should recur, we must see it slightly differently since we have changed, however slightly, since the previous encounter with that sensation. Our perspective is altered, our consciousness is not the same from one moment to the next; at the very least, the previous moment has elapsed and a new one has succeeded it. The relations are apprehended somewhat differently from the fresh perspective. The sense of sameness which we nonetheless experience has to be accounted for in order to understand how the same object can emerge from non-identical sensations being present to a constantly modified brain.

The principle to which James appeals in order to account for our knowledge about things as distinct from constantly changing acquaintance with them is that "the same matters can be thought of in successive portions of the mental stream, and some of these portions can know that they mean the same matters which the other portions meant" (459). In other words, "the mind can always intend, and know when it intends, to think of the Same" (459). The sense of sameness or identity of objects is a necessary condition for consciousness and knowledge as we know them. The subjective sense of sameness, that the identical person can perceive various sensations, has been the basis for many philosophers' explanation of how the world hangs together.

The sense of identity of the known object would perform the same function without having to assume subjective identity. A sense of personal identity alone could not give us an organized consciousness instead of chaos had we not the intention of thinking the same things over and over again.

So far, no assertions have been made concerning the objective identity of anything in the world. It has only been claimed that the mind is so structured that it thinks a unity, whether or not there is one. The mind continually uses the notion of sameness in order to make sense of its experience, but this psychological necessity does not necessarily correspond to anything in the world. In order for our experience to be what it is, the mind must continually utilize the notion of sameness or identity. This is a psychological fact about the structure of our mind and the nature of our experience and not a metaphysical fact about the world. Whether or not identity is true of anything, we are not deceived that we intend to think things as identical. This law of the constancy of our meanings, subjective though it is, comprises the most important feature of our mental structure (460). "The function by which we thus identify a numerically distinct and permanent subject of discourse is called *conception*" (461).

PASSIVE RECEPTION OF STIMULI
VERSUS CREATIVE RESPONSE

In the final chapter of the second volume of *The Principles of Psychology* James seeks to clarify an issue about which he has been disconcertingly vague in his discussion of the constitution of objects and relations in consciousness up to this point. This concerns the evaluation of the relative priority or inferiority of the configuration of relations and things in the outward environment in relation to the organization of sensations by the mind. James approaches this problem through trying to account for the mind's tendency to think of and react upon various sensations in fairly stereotyped ways, even when encountered for the first time. He is concerned to account for necessary propositions and for those experiential propositions which, while not logically necessary, are found to be invariant. He sides with those who would argue for the *a priori* structure of the mind against those empiricists who would hold that conscious interaction with the environment is sufficient to account for any structures of knowledge common to all men. But although he agrees on the whole with the facts that

18

support the *a priori* position, he disagrees as to their transcendental status, and substitutes instead a naturalistic view of their cause.

James holds that all schools of thought agree that the elementary qualities, such as hot, blue, pleasure, sound, etc., are innate or *a priori* in that they are properties of our subjective nature, even though they may need an experiential process to awaken them to consciousness (II, 618). The origin of these elements is not at issue, but their forms of combination. The empiricists insist that the order of combination which they exhibit in nature accounts for the order of the subjective impressions which mirror them, while the a priorists hold that some forms of combination, at least, are predetermined in such a way that the impressions of the external world could not account for them. What is in dispute is whether the mind has an organic mental structure independently of any experience, experience being defined as something foreign which impresses us, either spontaneously or as a result of some action on our part.

Impressions so affect us that their spatial order and temporal sequence impress their arrangements on the mental images of things. "To uniform outer coexistences and sequences correspond constant conjunctions of ideas, to fortuitous coexistences and sequences casual conjunctions of ideas" (II, 619). In *The Principles of Psychology* James still uses the model of images mediating between external reality and the mind; in his later writings he discards this fiction. The trains of regular or fortuitous sequences form our ideas of constant or casual conjunctions, respectively, which soon become so habitual that we cannot even conceive of reality in any other way than that which it originally and continuously exhibits. In these spatial and temporal conjunctions of things the order of nature is the true cause of our forms of thought and, thus, experience of these indispensable conditions of all further learning are experientially and not mentally based. However, all the connections in our mind are not so derived, as will be shown.

There are two ways in which changes are brought about in the mind, that is to say, two modes of origin of brain structure. On the one hand, natural agents produce perceptions which take cognizance of their own formation, and on the other hand, perceptions are caused which have no relation to their source of origin. The former case is experience proper in 'which the order of the experience itself is what is learned, the 'inner relation' corresponding to the 'outer relation' which produced it, "by remembering and knowing the latter" (II, 625). Natural objects, impressed on the brain through the senses, "in the

19

strict sense of the word give it *experience*, teaching it by habit and association what is the order of their ways" (II, 626). In the case of 'unconscious' perceptual origin, the mind acquires a new disposition through a natural agency which leaves no clue to the conscious mind of the manner in which it produces its effects. These natural agents, such as quinine and microbes, also modify the brain, but impress on it no cognition of themselves. Only those natural and physical processes which consciously influence the mental organism and are the objects as well as the subjects of their effects will henceforth be termed experience.

Although impressions of external objects are needed to activate the categories, simple mental duplication of the outer world cannot account for them, even though this suggestion is vague enough to sound plausible. The mere existence of things to be known is not sufficient to bring about a knowledge of them (II, 630). The more general discoveries are more often the result of lucky guesses or hypothetical constructs, which only afterwards are found to have a correlate in reality. The most likely hypothesis to account for the original elements of consciousness, such as sensation, time, space, resemblance, difference, and other relations, is that they were originally accidental morphological processes, engendered for no particular reason, which were subsequently found to be of great utility in handling ordinary experience. Rather than being immediate derivatives of the sensible presence of objects, they were probably pure idiosyncrasies fitted by good luck to take cognizance of objects. These mental duplicates of outer objects do not even resemble the objects which they allow us to know, their subjective characteristics depend more on the nature of the brain and sensory receptors than on something intrinsic to the object as such. Even though James included time and space along with other original elements of consciousness as accounted for by accidental morphology, he insists that they differ from the other categories in that they are impressed from without and are literal copies of external relations (II, 632).

A large part of our thinking consists of mere habits, fashioned from external things, space and time preeminently, but also the effects of neighborhood in time and space, e.g., that fire burns and water wets, that glass refracts and fish live in water. Thus, "an immense number of our mental habitudes, many of our abstract beliefs, and all our ideas of concrete things, and of their ways of behavior" are due to the passive receptivity of the mind, servilely copying what is presented to it (II, 632). Other images, although derived from images originally impressed on the mind by outer stimuli, are not congruent with forms as they exist in reality because of various associations and secondary combinations, such as the forms of judgment due to the activity of the mind, including memory, expectation, doubt, belief, and denial.

After a careful review of the material covered so far, it can only be concluded that James is fundamentally contradictory as to the genesis of the elementary mental categories as presented on pages 629-633 in *The Principles of Psychology*, II. Within a few paragraphs he calls these elementary categories idiosyncrasies, spontaneous variations in no way derivative from external objects, and literal copies of relations impressed on us from without. This fundamental ambiguity, nowhere more starkly juxtaposed than in these pages, will return to plague him when he adopts the clearly philosophical mode of discourse in his later writings.

ORIGINAL CHAOS VERSUS STRUCTURE

James is much more consistent and his insights are more seminal in his explanation of the genesis of the natural sciences. He clearly realized that the passive reception of empirical images is of a different order entirely from that which obtains in scientific thinking. The order of scientific thinking does not duplicate the order of reality nor the manner of its reception by us, but selects and emphasizes what it will. What actually exists is a totality, with each part contemporaneous and as important as every other part. But we cannot think or experience this totality in its all-at-oneness. "What we experience, what *comes before us*, is a chaos of fragmentary impressions interrupting each other; what we *think* is an abstract system of hypothetical data and laws" (II, 634). This theorizing or conceptualizing faculty does not record sensorial images but actively selects purposes which are not derived from nature but from our own emotional and practical subjectivity. We remodel the order of our experience by transforming the world of our impressions into a subjectively satisfying world, the world of our conceptions, for no other motive than the interests of our volitional nature.

Sensorial impressions come to us in an order foreign to our own interests. Not being able to imagine it as it is, we break the given order, which appears to us as chaotic disorder, and select items that interest us and arrange them in sequences and conjunctions that allow us to minimize accidental disruptions, pick out disguised tendencies, and maximize control of future liabilities. The world as it is given to us at any moment is an utter chaos, so it is no wonder that "we have no organ or faculty to appreciate the simply given order" (II, 635,

n. 4). The real world as it is now is the sum total of all that is going on in the whole universe, from the most minute molecular movement to the most distant galactic explosion. Such a cross-section of all actual things and events present everywhere is literally unthinkable, even though it is the real order of the world. We can only understand anything by getting away from everything and breaking the totality down into manageable groupings, such as are designated by the interests paramount in art, history, and science. We can only feel at home in the universe by ignoring most of what is there and by imposing on it our own idiosyncracies.

If accepted, this argument for the understanding of an otherwise chaotic world by the imposition of subjectively motivated interests should effectively eliminate all correspondence theories of truth along with the copy theory of the genesis of elementary mental categories. There could be no possibility of discovering the real relations which exist in the world, since if there were any, they would not be accessible to us otherwise than as an all-at-oneness. If it is granted that we sense only a chaos of fragmentary impressions in an order entirely foreign to our subjective interests, then none of the categories, including space and time, could mirror experience, let alone be derived from experience. It seems that in moving from the passive reception of sense impressions to the level of conceptual thought James has deepened the contradiction and created an unresolvable dilemma: either sensorial impressions impress us with their space and time order or else they exhibit only chaos; either subjective or perceptive space and time mirror the real order of the world and conceptual thought would merely explicate that order, or else the real order of the world is chaotic and space and time are as subjectively imposed upon the world as are the more elegantly worked out fictions of science.

In *The Principles of Psychology* this glaring inconsistency stands unresolved. It should be pointed out, though, that one part of James's explanation of the empirical categories does not contradict the scientific view just presented. It will be recalled that he rejected the notion of an outer world building up a mental duplicate of itself and claimed that the mere existence of things to be known is not sufficient to bring about a knowledge of them. Idiosyncrasy, not mental malleability, is responsible for the sensible categories. He only contradicted himself insofar as he exempted space and time relations from this general pattern, after having included them. The privileged status of space and time is asserted, but no compelling arguments are brought forward to show why they should not be treated in the same manner as the other original elements of consciousness.

In explicating the scientific perspective James continues the metaphor of an original chaos and a humanly imposed order. We impose on the chaos of impressions relations which were never derived therefrom (mathematical, biochemical theories, etc.) and isolate some relations as essential and law-like, ignoring all the ones that do not fit into this pattern. The relations that are thus isolated are essential, but only for our purposes. Change that purpose and other relations hitherto ignored would emerge as essential. The purpose of science could be said to be conceptual simplicity and foresight, and "the miracle of miracles, a miracle not yet exhaustively cleared up by any philosophy, is that the given order lends itself to the remodelling" (II, 635, n. †). Whether our subjective ends are esthetic, moral, practical, or scientific, our projections on the world yield results, although why nature's own order should thus be malleable to our interests remains a mystery.[10] A careful consideration of the genesis and nature of scientific theory should convince anyone that it could not possibly derive from mere observation of nature or experience in the ordinary sense. The formulation of scientific conceptions is comparable to flashes of poetic insight, the only difference being that the scientific hypotheses can be verified or falsified. This procedure, though, is only a condition of their acceptance, not an account of their genesis.

Although James does not explicitly say so, the pattern of his explanations would permit the suggestion that the over-abundance and richness of the relations in nature and not their paucity explain why subjective interests identify real currents. Other descriptions would also be adequate; we emphasize the ones we do instead of others for our own reasons, but these ultimately work only if they happen to coincide with one of the innumerable possibilities of nature. The questions should be raised as to whether there can be real possibilities in nature without real relations, and if real relations are given, then why not say that we can passively know them according to a correspondence theory of truth? Science would be a discipline of mere observation and description rather than one of hypothesis and confirmation. These questions are taken up in subsequent chapters, which will draw on James's later works.

Two assumptions can be made in the light of these early remarks of James on science that could possibly resolve the dilemma and still leave James in possession of the field. The first is that there are so many relations in nature, even contradictory ones, that there is no way to simply determine the relations or order of nature.[11] But too many relations in nature have about the same logical status as no relations in nature in that nothing can be solved by mere appeal to the given. This is because, according to the former, other relations, even contradictory ones, are also given depending on what is sought, and according to the latter, there are not any relations simply given which can be appealed to. However, there remains a logical distinction between the two positions in that, when some relation is proposed and it works, James can say it works because the relation is really given in nature. Hence, he thinks of himself as a philosophical realist. This doctrine of real relations is indispensable for James's claim of confirmation or refutation by experience. The "realism" is of a peculiar kind, though, in that the simply given order is disorder as far as we are concerned. Also, the objection can still be made to this assumption that it is vacuous, since innumerable relations are logically identical with no relations. This brings us to our second assumption, which is that the initiator or discoverer of relations himself influences the relations to be posited or discovered, which are nonetheless really given, but only as tendencies and not as fully constituted relations. It should also be recalled that for James there are no subjective or objective goals as such and that what we consider subjective or objective is ultimately a matter of preference. This assumption, which promises to be more fruitful than the previous one, will be worked out in the course of developing James's later comments on relations.

The relations science works with are not copied from nature but are worked out by ignoring most of experience and substituting precisely defined conditions for those given. The underlying hypothesis which allows science to operate at all, the principle of the uniformity of nature, has to be accepted despite, not because of, appearances. According to James the conviction of the truth of this assumption is more akin to religious faith than to assent to reasoned arguments. No such general laws can be read from nature, the only literal associations which nature presents are those of the proximate laws of nature and the associated sensorial impressions already mentioned (II, 637).[12] These empirical truths are the touchstones for the theoretical achievements of science. Unless scientific truths harmonize with these simpler truths, which arise in a passive associative way, they have to be given up. Laboratory experiments do not so much reveal new laws or truths as confirm what has already been conjectured. The confirmation or rejection takes place under artificially constructed conditions. "Instead of the experiences engendering the

24

'inner relations,' the inner relations are what engender the experiences here" (II, 138). Experiments are applicable to and refer to phenomena, but the phenomena themselves are part of artificially constructed conditions. What formally makes a scientific hypothesis law-like is that it states a regularity or stability in the observed phenomena. But the phenomena observed are not everyday events.

The order of nature is altered because we find other relations more interesting than the mere repetition of space and time conjunctions that nature offers us. The materials nature supplies can be most completely and easily translated into scientific forms, most slowly and least satisfactorily into ethical forms, and more readily into esthetic forms (II, 640). This intriguing insight is not carried further, beyond the statement that the translation remains an always unfinished task, since the perceptive order does not give way, nor is the right conceptual substitute produced, at our mere command.

Having indicated the relation of the natural sciences to experience, strictly so called, James goes on to delineate the pure sciences as those that express the results of comparison only. Comparison is not gathered from the order of nature but is attributable to the activity of the mind, what James calls the "house-born portions of our mental structure" (II, 641). The body of propositions which form the pure sciences do not derive from experience but dictate to it. The relations of similarity and difference are independent of any spatial or temporal sequence which we experience. But the advocates of persistent outer relations hold that the propositions of pure science are due to the invariance of nature, which has gradually built up mental duplicates. According to this interpretation the necessary forms of thought are only reflections of the fact that certain outer relations have always held. The reason that we have always found necessary relations is either a subjective one, that our mind is so constructed that sameness and differences are invariably associated with certain sensations, such as black and white, or an objective one, that the differences always appear as such outside the mind, which only reflects them.

The subjective reason undercuts experience by explaining outer frequency by inner structure and not inner structure by outer frequency (II, 643). The objective reason merely reiterates the truism that if there are outer differences the mind must know them, which does not explain anything, but simply appeals to the fact that there are similarities and differences and that the mind knows them. James does not attempt to give an account of the origin of necessary relations, but points out that necessary forms of thought have arisen, we know not how, and conjectures that they did so because of some

25

development of the brain and nervous system. We know that black and white differ, and always will differ, not because of some examination of many samples of black and white, but because what we mean by black differs from what we mean by white even if no samples of white or black could be found in the world. Those propositions expressing space and time relations will be called empirical propositions and those which express the results of comparison will be called rational propositions, since to ascertain the former, experience must be consulted, while to ascertain the latter an inspection of the ideas suffices.

James thus agrees that many necessary and eternal relations obtain among the conceptions of the mind, forming determinate systems, independent of the order of frequency of the original conceptions in space and time (II, 661). These have traditionally been designated as innate or *a priori* bodies of truth, although these labels have engendered so much controversy that James hesitates to use them, even though admitting their appropriateness. The eternal truths which these conceptual categories embody do not in turn reflect extramental being. They are subjective categories which form an ideal network which may or may not capture some of the features of reality, although by their use we hope to discover realities. The given structure of the mind means that certain objects, taken in certain ways, will always yield the same results and that no other considerations or results are possible, given the same objects (II, 676). The causes of our mental structure are most likely due to some development of our nervous system and cannot be accounted for by interacting experiences since we can give no account of their origin. While not calling them innate, James, in the last paragraph of the book, also links up with the peculiarities of our nervous structure the genesis of our interests, our ability to apprehend schemes of relations, and even the elementary relations themselves of time, space, difference, similarity, and simple feelings (II, 688). He claims that the origin of none of these can be accounted for, although he has just finished making extensive suggestions concerning their origins, distinguishing between the experiential and the mind-originating ones.

The different levels of relations, insofar as they can be pieced together from the discussions in *The Principles of Psychology*, can be divided into two groupings depending on whether the mind is more active or passive *vis-à-vis* experience. The first group, involving rational propositions, consists of (1) the pure sciences, in which the mind engenders ideal mathematical relations, and (2) the natural sciences, which formulate more general laws and the elementary laws of mechanics, physics, chemistry, etc. The second group, involving empirical propositions, consists of (a) the proximate laws of nature and the habitudes of concrete things, which are engendered by the associations of the given order of nature, and (b) the impressions of space and time, which mirror the real space and time relations. Only the second group of relations arise from "experience strictly so called."

Rephrasing the Problem and Projecting Solutions

The questions raised at the beginning of this chapter in regard to the constitution of objects and relations can best be dealt with from the perspective of James's later works, which will be taken up next. A problem has arisen in explicating those themes in *The Principles of Psychology* which are relevant to the later elaboration of the doctrine of relations. The problem concerns the dilemma raised by James's insistence on two contradictory primordial realities: chaotic sensations and a given space-time order. Quite divergent conclusions follow depending on which of these two is the more fundamental reality. If chaos is fundamental, then either selective interest or accidental morphological changes must be invoked to make order out of it. In either case, the order is supplied by a person, through the constructive activity of a knower, and would be labeled *a priori* in the sense of not being derived from experience. If the order imposed on the chaos is due to selective interest then the *a priori* would have the status of a hypothetical proposition of the form "If . . . then. . . ." If consistencies are interesting, then regularities will be observed, but if moral considerations are paramount, then the universe will include moral phenomena, and so on. If the order imposed on the chaos is due to physical development, then a universal, unchanging, and necessary *a priori* could be operative, or at least, a structurally enduring *a priori*, subject to evolutionary or biological change. If, on the other hand, a given order is fundamental, then the knower would be primarily passive, receiving mirror images or impressions, and only secondarily active, changing and manipulating the original order through associations in order to come up with new combinations. Unfortunately, James has espoused all of these alternatives at one point or other! We must count as evidence for a given empirical order both his assertions that relations are a matter of direct particular experience and his insistence that space and time are given to us to be literally copied. We must count as evidence for an originary chaos his proposal of the vague as a category, the selectivity of the mind,

27

the mind intending the same, even though never confronted with identical sensations, and science as an abstract system of hypothetical data and laws by which the chaos of fragmentary impressions are interpreted.

A possible resolution of this dilemma is hinted at in the distinction made between knowledge of acquaintance and knowledge-about. The more elementary sort of knowledge, knowledge of acquaintance, concerns the vaguely intuited relations of the fringe. This mere acquaintance with many relations and objects is an awareness of everything at once in the unarticulated chaos of immediate presentation. The chaos is a result of an over-abundance of relations, which are too numerous to be grasped, rather than an absence of relations. Knowledge-about complements this first awareness by selecting out of the chaos some of the relations according to design by conceptualizing them. But is it possible to be given relations so vague as to be chaotic and still claim that we have direct particular experience of relations? It would seem that absolute chaos would logically rule out any awareness of the relations of objects. A more modest claim of a limited or quasi-chaos, such as an assertion of vagueness, would allow for the awareness of some order, even though that order may not be perfectly distinct, as when we look through a camera that is slightly out of focus. Another approach would be to assert a primordially chaotic situation brought about as a result of the over-abundance, not the paucity, of relations. The proof of the presence of any given set of relations would lie in the success or failure of some selective interest. What would otherwise count as the criteria for the success of a scheme, whether scientific, esthetic, or moral, unless some schemes worked and others did not? If some schemes do not work, and some demonstrably do not, then the given must not be completely malleable, but has its own resistances, tendencies, and relations.

A resolution of these difficulties is possible within the proposals made by James, if we eliminate some of his assertions in favor of others which can be more consistently asserted. The claim of a direct apprehension of a distinct space and time order would have to be dropped in favor of various times and spaces depending on the selective interest brought to bear, i.e., the model, predisposition, or frame of reference brought to experience. A quasi-chaos would have to be substituted for an absolute primordial chaos, and the immediate perception of relations and objects, just as they are, would have to be eliminated in favor of the distinct perception of objects and relations at the later stage of knowledge-about, since the earlier stage of knowledge of acquaintance is an unfocused awareness of tendency, resistence, and uncoordinated sensations.[13] A strict empiricism of individual plural facts giving rise to a unified theory is untenable on the assumption of knowledge of acquaintance, according to which the given is only vaguely apprehended, but apprehended as a much-at-once, nonetheless, and not as single discrete bits of sense data. A modified or radical empiricism must be asserted, instead, in which knowledge-about is joined to knowledge of acquaintance, and both fringe and focus are important.

It remains to be seen whether the more consistent alternative in each of these pairs was chosen or emphasized by James in his later writings. Even within the framework of selected proposals some problems remain which will eventually have to be taken up. Since knowledge-about involves the imposition of categories, how far are the categories morphological and therefore necessary and not under conscious control? In what sense are they due to the 'funded' character of experience and thus reflect previous interpretations, and how far are they due to selective interest, and therefore purposive, but still arbitrary as far as given relations are concerned? Furthermore, is everyone's selective interest absolutely unique, or does it follow certain patterns, such as ethical self-creation, the body as center of interest, or cultural conditioning?

CHAPTER TWO

AN ORIGINALLY CHAOTIC
VERSUS AN ORDERED, COHERENT WORLD

INTRODUCTION

THE CHOICE between an originally chaotic or an ordered, coherent world was left unresolved in *The Principles of Psychology*. James takes up the problematic again in *Essays in Radical Empiricism* and incorporates some of the ambiguity into his elaboration of the doctrine of pure experience. In *Essays in Radical Empiricism* he still tends to speak of chaos as though it were absolute and about continuity-relations as though they were equally unyielding. However, he also gives hints as to a possible reconciliation. The status of relations as it emerges in the doctrine of experience is intimately linked to the theme of chaos. Consequently, I will draw together those remarks James makes about chaos to see if they form a unified view, to see to what extent he still holds to the explanation of chaos given in *The Principles of Psychology*, and to show how the theme of chaos functions when the model of pure experience replaces the model of the stream of consciousness. Before taking up his remarks in *Essays in Radical Empiricism*, it is important to recall what has already been elaborated in *The Principles of Psychology*.

THE STATE OF THE QUESTION IN
The Principles of Psychology

James assumed an ordered, coherent universe in order to explain empirical propositions, which consist of the proximate laws of nature and the habitudes of concrete things as well as spatial and temporal relations. These empirical propositions are engendered by the associations of the given order of nature, which are simply copied or mirrored. Only when explaining rational propositions, which comprise the natural and pure sciences, does James introduce a primal, chaotic reality. These rational propositions are not part of experience, but only because reality as we experience it is not ordered into neat systems of data and laws. On the contrary, sensorial impressions appear to us so chaotically disordered that we can only grasp them at all by ignoring the experiential evidence and substituting for it an order congenial to our interests. In *The Principles of Psychology* James does not reconcile nor seek to diminish the inconsistency of these two contradictory views of the manner in which reality affects us. In the one context the passive reception of empirical images yields spatial and temporal relations, in the other context it yields utter chaos.

I offered a tentative resolution to this contradiction by stressing the multiplicity and abundance of relations, so that both temporal-spatial and scientifically interesting relations could be said to be given in experience, but could be recognized only insofar as they were sought. Selective interest, not the overwhelming variety of sensory impressions, would thus be determinate in disclosing what is given. However, the acceptance of this hypothesis would entail abandoning James's distinction of an absolute dichotomy between empirical and rational propositions, his criteria of an appeal to absolute space and time for the truth or falsity of scientific propositions, the immediate knowledge of distinct relations, and the total chaos of first impressions. Before seeing in what direction James moves in regard to the order-chaos dilemma, how well he faced up to the disparity, and whether the hypothetical solution squares with his later thought, a few more descriptive characteristics of chaos should be recalled from *The Principles of Psychology*.

Scientific thinking ignores the order in which sensory impressions reach us, as well as their manner of reception, because the sense images available at any one moment are so overwhelmingly numerous that they could not all elicit equal attention. Or, to put it another way, if we would relax our selective interest, the totality of images present are so numerous as to appear chaotic, somewhat as the movements of an ant-heap appear random and chaotic until one or another ant is selectively scrutinized and the purposiveness of his movements noted.[1] The all-at-oneness of sensory impressions appears to us as a fragmentary chaos since we have no organ to appreciate such an undifferentiated simultaneity. We react to this chaos by selecting items or relations subjectively interesting to us and remodeling the order of our experience. Why the world of impressions should thus yield to our manipulation is left as a mystery by James; it is sufficient for his purposes to point out that it does. Our esthetic, moral, practical, and scientific projections on the world bring to light relations and data which would be otherwise unrecognized and concomitantly ignore relations which do not fit the prescribed pattern. With each change of the conceptual framework bits of relations and terms fall kaleidoscopically into place. James recognizes that scientific theory cannot be said to be derivable from observation or experience in any meaningful sense of derivation, but does not yet draw the further conclusion that this must be true of all our human projects.

FURTHER DEVELOPMENTS IN
Essays in Radical Empiricism

In *Essays in Radical Empiricism* James realizes that spatial and temporal relations are not immune to the judgment that the universe is to a large extent chaotic. These relations have no privileged position in respect to the arbitrariness of the world as it appears. In labeling the universe chaotic he now means that it resists all attempts at unification whether by a single principle or a unified system. It should be noted that with this shift of meaning, chaos as a description of a field of consciousness has been de-emphasized and instead is used to explain why no single rational explanation of the world is possible. The world appears chaotic to a great extent: "No one single type of connexion runs through all the experiences that compose it" (*E.R.E.*, 24). No matter which relation is singled out, many experiences can be found in which that relation does not hold. The space relation works well in most perceptual experience but does not hold for conceptualization or for connecting minds; causes and purposes unify certain delimited situations and are inapplicable in many others; the relation to oneself does not join us to other selves. No relationship that unifies various experiences has been found which unifies all experience whatever. Other experiences are always left over which appear chaotic when judged by their coherence with the given relation. For all the experiences which are shared in that they terminate in common perceptions, there are as many left over which do not.

Rationalism emphasizes the universal aspects of our experiences, while empiricism emphasizes the discontinuities. Both can point to experiences which corroborate their claims because the universe is variously related and these relations can be emphasized and exaggerated by ignoring or considering as insignificant the discontinuities. The universe also exhibits enough situations that do not relate to each other to judge it as a "multiverse" of chaos by denying or ignoring the connections that do appear and emphasizing the many parts of experience that are related only extrinsically in that they are located with one another, but appear to have no more intimate relation. Radical empiricism is distinguished from both rationalism and empiricism by the fact that it accepts both the continuities and discontinuities on the same level. Both the relations and the discontinuity can be described, and it is a matter of emphasis or focus which comes to the fore. Within their proper range, definite descriptions can be given for both a continuous and a discontinuous universe.

James has thus made a significant distinction which goes far in clearing up the chaos versus order contradiction which he has thus far simply juxtaposed. Both order and chaos are originally given, depending on what point of view or context is emphasized. In a common sense, primarily perceptual, perspective, space and time, the habitudes of concrete things, and various related associations are given just as they appear and are uncritically accepted. From a scientific or theoretical point of view these simple experiences become problematic in that the model of perception as selective replaces the uncritical model of perception as a mere recording screen. The basis for this switch is that the original experience, antedating both perception and conception, or at the basis of both, is postulated to be an undifferentiated unity of thought and thing, of a much-at-oneness, of myriads of relations and relata not yet distinguished into this and that particular. Percepts are specific selections out of the tangled chaos, and the percepts thus habitually brought forth serve as the basis for the further, more conscious choices and combinations.[2] The universe is described as fundamentally chaotic in that no single principle or system successfully unifies it, but within any given context or point of view or selected experience, many relations and ordered groupings of things appear as immutably given. The particular perspective discloses, reveals, or allows for, certain groupings and no others as long as that perspective is adhered to. In a certain perspective space and time appear as given data with which various conceptual constructs such as formulas for architectural construction have to square in order to be accepted, while in another perspective something else, such as motion or simultaneity, serves as the basic data with which time and space, as conceptual constructs have to correlate.

James himself did not draw out the consequences of this distinction.

He speaks of accepting both the continuities and the discontinuities in a way which emphasizes the immutable givenness of certain relations almost as if these relations could force the creation of a context in which they would be recognized, rather than a specific context allowing for certain relations. James realized that the strength of his philosophical position depended on the denial of the extremes of asserting either the priority of arbitrary imposition of selective interest on a completely malleable manifold or the priority of immutable natures and intrinsic relations dictating to completely impressionable minds. In denying the one-sidedness of either position he tends to misleadingly overemphasize the contrary one. Still, James seems to hold that various continuities hold independently of any context or perspective.

Both percepts and concepts are in their immediacy undifferentiated bits of pure experience, as will be further developed under the theme of pure experience. The world of concepts, like the world of percepts, comes to us at first chaotically, and only later do lines of order get traced (*E.R.E.*, 9-10). Undifferentiated or chaotic bits of experience are single 'thats' not yet apprehended as any 'what'; according to their context one bit may act as an object, while in another context it may figure as a mental state. Taking concepts in their immediacy means ignoring their relation to possible perceptual experiences which they may be said to terminate in or, in a certain manner, represent. The lines of order, or relations, which may be traced in the originally chaotic experience depend on the point of view or interests we adopt; some groups of associates link themselves according to the relations engendered by association, other relations are those of personal biography and an impersonal objective world, whether spatial, temporal, mathematical, or whatever. "Here as elsewhere the relations are of course *experienced* relations, members of the same originally chaotic manifold of non-perceptual experience of which the related terms themselves are parts" (*E.R.E.*, 10, n.6). The same non-perceptual experience, like an identical perceptual experience, can be wholly objective or wholly subjective, depending on the context. The same experience tends to be counted twice, in one context figuring as an object or field of objects and in another context figuring as a state of mind. It is not both at once, but wholly one or the other, depending on the emphasis.

James suggests that a hypothesis that could explain how chaotic pure experiences gradually became differentiated into an orderly inner and outer world would involve showing how the quality of an experience, once active, became less so until it takes on the status of an inert or internal nature rather than that of a dynamic attribute (*E.R.E.*,

18). Accordingly, the psychical would be an evolutionary development from the physical, with the esthetic, moral, and emotional experiences serving as intermediaries, since their status is even now ambiguous. Sometimes this class of affective experiences is assigned a subjective value and at other times an objective one, depending on which aspect we want to emphasize.

The theme of the chaotic nature of experience in its immediacy is intimately related to the view of the world as pluralistic, to the affirmation of innumerable relations, and to the sense of activity, or fact of change. The pluralism of the world is seen by James as an *ad hoc* situation, in that the absolute unity of the world has not been experienced as yet. The pluralistic character of the world is not arrived at by stipulation but by defect, that is, until the unity of the world can be experienced and demonstrated, it cannot be assumed. Unifying factors do seem to be at work in that various trains of experience, hitherto unrelated, are seen to be conjoined as new scientific, esthetic, or moral perspectives reveal hitherto unrealized connections. New experiences constantly add to and transform earlier experiences. This characteristically optimistic outlook of James, however, is recognized for what it is: a mere hope that the world will someday be seen in its unified totality. What is asserted as actuality is a pluralistic world; any ultimate unity is for James a desirable goal but is proffered only as a possibility.[3]

Since experiences come on such an enormous scale, their relations are chaotically incommensurable when taken in their totality (*E.R.E.*, 65–66). Different groups of relations have to be sorted out of the mass in order to grasp any relations at all. As to how or why these primal experiences are constituted, and why the unselected nature of the relations is as given, or why relations eventually appear in a certain order and not another, James confesses to complete ignorance. This lack of theoretical daring is disappointing, especially since so many crucial issues turn upon the resolution of this state of affairs. The problem left thus summarily unresolved is the central one of reconciling chaotic experiences and incommensurable relations with ordered relations which become apparent when once they are selected out of the mass. Although James claims to have merely juxtaposed "a chaos of incommensurable relations" and experiences and relations that "get themselves made," he actually brought these two seemingly contradictory states of affairs into a more harmonious scheme than he admits. An extensive effort to resolve the dilemma can be found in his development of the theme of pure experience, which will be taken up in the next chapter.

That the universe we live in is chaotic also means that no part of experience has an unequivocal mental or physical status (*E.R.E.*, 70 ff.). Besides the ambiguous group of affections, emotions, and other appreciative perceptions which have already been mentioned, and which retain their ambiguity even in everyday expressions, the variety of relations and the many ways of taking them guarantees that sorting experiences into physical and mental is a precarious task and easily overturned. Not only are the relations given in experience confusingly numerous, the ways of appropriating those relations are equally numerous and sometimes contradictory. The essential part played by context in the sifting of the general chaos of our experiences into physical and mental has already been pointed out.

Activity is affirmed whenever something is going on; it is the "apprehension of something *doing*" (*E.R.E.*, 82). Bare activity, the expression of event or change, is a unique content of experience and not something added to it. The sense of activity is broadly synonymous with life itself, our own experience of life, first of all. "We *are* only as experients" (*E.R.E.*, 82). Experience is founded on the actuality of event or change. The chaotic character of pure experience when taken in its immediacy is only understandable on the basis of the fact of change. The original expression of change is chaotic. Only when an aspect of change has been assigned to an operator and another aspect designated as the event or action, does the originally chaotic situation become ordered and comprehensible. This is an enlargement of the field of experience, however, and not a reduction to a primal duality. In pure experience there is no inner duplicity, although there is a manifold; the separation into consciousness and content, into actor and act, comes by way of addition. That something is going on—but not what, how, or by whom—is immediately given. Three distinguishable activities can be noted: (1) the elementary activity best designated as the mere 'that' of experience, (2) the fact that something is going on, and (3) specifying this 'something' into two 'whats', namely, personal activity and an activity ascribed to objects (*E.R.E.*, 85–86, n.8).

At this crucial juncture James derives the notions of causal efficacy, of distinct agents, and of activity versus passivity, from the assertion that "in this actual world of ours, as it is given, a part at least of the activity comes with definite direction; it comes with desire and sense of goal" (*E.R.E.*, 82). Although this sounds like an example of continuities forcing themselves upon us outside of any specific context, a careful reading reveals that James is attempting to describe a particular class of contexts: that of activity situations. Whenever we call a certain context an activity, it will be seen on inspection to include some or all of these components: physical or mental agent, a goal or aimlessness, tendencies, resistances, effort, and will. The definite direction is found within the activity situation, whom or what it is attributable to cannot be decided beforehand, although James favors an explanation which emphasizes interaction on many levels, each contributing something, rather than a simplistic action-reaction formula.

RECAPITULATION AND PROJECTION

The introduction of the meaning of chaos as signifying that the universe cannot be unified within a single system, principle, or idea, has helped to clarify the exposition of chaos given in *The Principles of Psychology*. It is necessary to specify the context to bring order out of chaos, and the order engendered will vary with the context, since each context allows for the realization of some relations and prohibits others. The centrality of context to the theme of the chaotic nature of experience can serve to relate chaos to the allied themes of pluralism, multiple relations, and activity or change. These ideas cannot be developed, however, nor can this interconnection be explored outside of the more inclusive and fundamental doctrine of pure experience. It is necessary to give a more detailed explanation of the doctrine of pure experience and the status of relations before deciding whether the internal inconsistencies of the chaos versus order dilemma have finally been resolved.

CHAPTER THREE

THE EXPERIENCE OF RELATIONS AND THE POSTULATE OF PURE EXPERIENCE

INTRODUCTION

THE ASSERTION of the reality of relations, as a matter of direct particular experience, can be better understood when it is realized that James usually compares them to something else which is accepted as real or as a matter of experience. This is a significant clue to the status of relations: they are "just as much matters of direct particular experience, neither more so nor less so, than the things themselves" (*M.T.*, 7). The relations between things are as susceptible to direct observation as are the things, or terms, of the relation. This makes it incumbent on us to investigate James's explanation of our way of apprehending things in order to ascertain the status of things and to see what it means to say that they are experienced. Another way to formulate the proposition that relations are experienced is to say that the relations that connect experiences are themselves part of experience and "must be accounted as 'real' as anything else in the system" (*E.R.E.*, 22). Relations, just like anything else which can be called real, are considered real because of their place within a system or "philosophical arrangement." This does not mean that James ever held that experiences can be deduced from a universal system, but that the elements or parts of experience would have to be explained or systematized in such a way as to give equal status to terms and relations, since they are experienced in the same way and to the same degree. Radical empiricism is a description of things, not a logic-deductive system. This description, however, is not photographic or journalistic, but a taking account of experience by an explanation which makes sense of an otherwise inchoate situation.[1] In elucidating the status of relations, it is imperative to consider in some detail James's postulate of experience, since the two are interdependent. Indeed, if James's explanation of experience cannot be made sense of, then neither can his theory of relations.

THE PRIMACY OF PURE EXPERIENCE

In a common-sense point of view, 'thoughts' and 'things' are considered as referring to two different orders of reality, neither of which can be reduced to the other, but according to the pattern of which everything else can be classified. What is not mental is physical or some interaction of the two. Since the mental and the physical are taken to be irreducibly distinct, most philosophers have tried to relate the two in a coherent way. James first struggled with the dichotomy of things versus consciousness in his psychological studies. In his landmark work, *The Principles of Psychology*, he reluctantly allowed the dichotomy to stand. Later on, with more consistency, he abandoned this dualism.[2] What allows him to abandon consciousness as an equiprimordial entity along with physical things is his liberating hypothesis of pure experience.[3] "My thesis is that if we start with the supposition that there is only one primal stuff or material in the world, a stuff of which everything is composed, and if we call that stuff 'pure experience,' then knowing can easily be explained as a particular sort of relation towards one another into which portions of pure experience may enter" (*E.R.E.*, 4). This eliminates the need for thinking of consciousness as an entity, an "aboriginal stuff or quality of being" radically opposed to the "stuff" of physical things. Rather, consciousness is a notion used to indicate the function of knowing. That things get known is just as much part of experience as the existence of things, but the knowing process should not be conceived of as one entity—consciousness—reporting on another entity—physical things. The notion, consciousness, should be replaced by the function of knowing, in which portions of pure experience enter into various relationships and function in certain identifiable ways (*E.R.E.*, 4).[4]

The use of the words "stuff" and "material" in connection with pure experience is misleading. It is not a clay-like *materia prima* out of which other things are fashioned. In order to prevent misunderstanding James says later in the same essay, "there is no *general* stuff of which experience at large is made" (*E.R.E.*, 14). James always preferred a more concrete to a more abstract term and often leaves as an analogy insights which would have benefitted from a more precisely articulated formulation. James's thesis of "one primal stuff or material in the world" is meant as a counter-assertion to those who hold to an aboriginal dualism of consciousness. James is not asserting a meta-physical sub-stratum, but he is denying the subject-object distinction as irreducible. Pure experience is neither monistic nor dualistic; it is undifferentiated.

What should be noted in the given formulation of pure experience is that it is put forward as a supposition or hypothesis: "The principle of pure experience is also a methodical postulate" (*E.R.E.*, 81). This hypothesis gives a better account of experience, including the con-stitution of knowing, of subjects and objects, and of perception and conception, than the most prevalent alternate view, that consciousness is irreducibly dualistic, consisting of subject plus object (*E.R.E.*, 5). Although James's targets at this point are the so called neo-Kantians, his misunderstanding of the neo-Kantian, indeed, the Kantian posi-tion, renders his characterization of them innocuous. However, so many philosophers today begin their exposition with what can only be regarded as a parody of Kantian philosophy, and yet seem to make progress despite their misconstrual, that this misrepresentation on James's part cannot be held overly detrimental to his exposition. James puts forth the neo-Kantian view only as a contrast to highlight his own view and seems to have been aware that he was setting up, to a greater or lesser extent, a straw man. "Neo-Kantian" serves as a handy label for two assertions which James wants to refute: that consciousness is dualistically structured, and that we have an im-mediate intuition of consciousness.

Context Adds Individuation

The separation of experience into consciousness and content happens by way of addition, not subtraction (*E.R.E.*, 6–7). To one concrete part of experience are added other sets of experiences, so that what was once taken as undivided becomes separated into parts or terms, according to various functions or uses. James gives the example of paint which is just so much saleable matter in a shop, whereas that same paint on a canvas is an esthetic feature in a picture. The color patch admired as contributing to a composition is not the same thing as a certain quantity of saleable material and yet both originated in the same paint can. Add to the paint in the can another context, in this case an artist's studio or art gallery, and something new emerges; something has been added to the original situation. Quantitatively the same paint is involved, but its function has changed so much that we no longer call this particular quantity of paint by the same name nor do we consider it to be the same thing in both contexts, e.g., we no longer refer to the paint patch in the picture as saleable matter, since it is no longer useful to anyone as such, i.e., it can no longer be applied at will to some task; it has been literally hardened into one particular function as a part of the given painting.

Context likewise determines whether any given undivided portion of experience shall be counted as knower or known. In one context of associates the same experience plays the part of knower, of consciousness, whereas in another context it figures as the thing known, as object (E.R.E., 7). The same experience can figure as both thought and thing simultaneously, depending on which context is taken, and so can be labeled as both subjective and objective. In this account the subject-object dualism is acknowledged, but as a secondary phenomenon which, as an affair of relations, falls outside the individual experience and thus can be particularized and defined. Public criteria can thus be derived for objectivity since the relations which determine the status of objectivity are not a matter of solely personal experience, but are commonly identifiable.

In analyzing perceptual experience it will be acknowledged that the physical objects of the environing world, with their actual and potential physical relations, are at the same time the perceptions experienced as belonging to the experiencing subject. The paradox of how one reality can be in two places at once, both in outer space and in a person's mind, is analogous to the puzzle of how one identical point can be on two lines (E.R.E., 8). Just as a point at an intersection figures as belonging wholly and undividedly to two lines, the 'pure experience' of a given room lies at an intersection of processes connecting it with different groups of associates, so that it can be said to belong wholly to either group, while being numerically the same experience. The identical experience has many diverse relations, which can be variously traced, depending on which context of associates is taken up—the field of consciousness or personal biography as one process and the physical room or history of the place as the other. The physical and mental operations, though due to the same original experience, form incompatible groups, so that what is true of the events or personal biography is false if attributed to the thing experienced, and vice versa.

In their immediacy the world of concepts, like the world of percepts, are bits of experience, single *thats*, which soon get identified as objects in one context and as mental states in another (*E.R.E.*, 9). Just as in perceptual experience, the chaos of experiences soon gets sorted into various relations according to which group of associates is chosen. The numerically identical non-perceptual experience can be treated according to one context as an object or field of objects and in another context as a state of mind. Experience in its pure state, as isolated, is not divided into consciousness and object of consciousness; this subjective-objective dichotomy is a functional attribute only, determined retrospectively according to which context is being considered. "The instant field of the present is at all times what I call the 'pure' experience" (*E.R.E.*, 13). This plain, unqualified existence is only virtually or potentially either subject or object. Conscious experience is an addition to 'pure' experience, which is not made of any general stuff. Pure experience consists of just what appears, of *that*, of space, intensity, heaviness or what have you. "Experience is only a collective name for all these sensible natures, and save for time and space (and, if you like, for 'being') there appears no universal element of which all things are made" (*E.R.E.*, 15).

Thought and thing are not so heterogeneous as is commonly assumed, but have some categories in common. The adequate mental picture of any object has the same extension, for example, and whether physical or mental is determined by context and the relations which inhere in that context (*E.R.E.*, 15–16). In the general chaos of experiences one group of experiences always acts energetically. The stable part of the "experience-chaos" are the objects of the physical world, according to which consequences always accrue. Perceptual experiences are the original strong experiences, to which are added conceptual experiences, and together these comprise the physical world. Around this core of reality mere fancies float, which are distinguished from the physical world in that rules are strictly adhered to in the physical reality. Unless more carefully elaborated, this rule which James advocates as being a criterion to judge between physical and mental will not do because logical rules are notoriously exacting while many physical attributes and consequences are perfectly haphazard. The other criterion of acting energetically is countermanded by his analysis of activity and causality, given later in *Essays in Radical Empiricism* (especially page 92), wherein causality, real physical effectuation, is brought about through the energy of sustaining, persevering, and achieving an intention.

James realized this inconsistency (*E.R.E.*, 92–93, n. 9), but denied that it followed, because mental activity series energize by other parts of their nature than do the physical series. The thought of purpose, which energizes mentally, plays absolutely no part in the physical series. Although James admits that this needs careful working out, he does not do so, and the peculiar criterion given for sorting physical and mental, i.e., the fact that mental states energize purposely whereas physical states energize according to necessary consequences, remains extremely problematical, in that in both cases it is a mental judgment or interpretation—not an incontrovertible fact—that is being appealed to in stating that mental activities are purposeful (and therefore changeable) whereas physical ones are necessary (and therefore invariant). The counter-instance, just referred to, of exact logical rules and haphazard physical events, such as accidents, illustrates the weakness of the criterion.

James gives other criteria for distinguishing the physical world from the mental one, but he first stresses that consciousness and matter do not arise from two different sources (*E.R.E.*, 270). Originally simple experiences become physical or mental in their entirety by way of addition, not by way of subtracting or ignoring half of a supposedly double composition. Among the various criteria given for distinguishing the physical from the mental are these: "Forasmuch as experiences extend in time, enter into relations of physical influence, reciprocally split, warm, illuminate, etc., each other, we make of them a field apart which we call the physical world. On the other hand, forasmuch as they are transitory, physically inert, with a succession which does not follow a predetermined order but seems rather to obey emotive fancies, we make of them another field which we call the psychical world" (*E.R.E.*, 270). Besides the fact that James has already said that the relations to time of thoughts and things are identical (*E.R.E.*, 15), all the criteria for physical things beg the question because they include an appeal to the physical as already known as part of the criteria for deciding what is physical. Instead of being criteria for the physical, they are themselves physical descriptions, i.e., as criteria *for* the physical he gives physical descriptions which would themselves have to have other criteria for being physical. For instance, he says that the physical can be distinguished from the mental if it is recognized as entering into "relations of physical influence." But it is precisely the problem of providing a rule to identify the physical that is at issue. The recognition of a relation as physical does not tell us why it is physical and not mental. Furthermore, the criteria for the mental world are not exclusive and would apply equally well to the physical world. The physical field is as transitory as the mental field, changing all the while we ourselves change, and the appeal to its "physical inertness" again begs the question.

In the elaboration of pure experience James's failure to come up with hard and fast criteria for distinguishing the physical from the mental is regrettable, but superfluous to his central insight. Common sense is hopelessly dualistic and anyone can come up with criteria for distinguishing the physical from the mental in an uncritical way, sufficient for ordinary purposes. James's brilliant insight is that "thoughts and things are absolutely homogeneous as to their material, and that their opposition is only one of relation and of function" (*E.R.E.*, 69). The mental is distinguished from the physical according to their operations and practical results and not because of some essential difference between the two. Pure experience is not a composition of thought and thing, but an identical experience which can stand either for a fact of consciousness or for a physical reality depending on which context is taken. The psychical and the physical are so little heterogeneous that if all explanatory inventions which attempt to account for physical phenomena in terms of scientific theory are discarded, the immediate sensible reality and the sensation which we have of it are absolutely identical at the time the sensation occurs. "Reality is apperception itself" (*E.R.E.*, 263).

Our sensations of things are not inner duplicates of them, but the things themselves as they are presented to us. Any claims for the private life of things, hypothesized to account for what we do perceive, remain of necessity mere guesses and artificial constructs. The present actuality of things which we perceive, their public life, must remain the touchstone for all theoretical constructions made concerning them, and this actuality is numerically one with a certain part of our inner life. In this portion of experience known as sense perception, subject and object fuse in the fact of presentation, the same experience existing as an ultimate *that* or fact of being in the first instance, and in its other context, the same *that* figures as knowledge of the thing (*E.R.E.*, 100).

The central point of the pure experience theory is that 'outer' and 'inner' are names for two groups into which we sort experiences according to the way in which they act upon their neighbors (*E.R.E.*, 70). Something is grouped as an idea or a sensation according to the different type of interrelation into which it enters. We can imagine a world in which the physical or mental status of any bit of experience would be unequivocal, but the world we live in is more chaotic. Subjectivity and objectivity are not attributes of a primeval experience, but rather the results of a later classification. This classification is a result of our interests and temporary purposes; according to the context, different sets of relations come into play. The affections and emotional experiences are good examples of ambiguous experiences that have resisted being hardened into the either-or mold of subjective or objective. In practical life no urgent need has compelled us to label them as exclusively mental or physical facts, so they remain equivocal. Every experience, however complex, at the moment of its actual presence, is at first a 'pure' fact, and simply 'is'; only later is it confined to this thing or that. We relocate experiences and group them with different sets of associates according to our practical or intellectual ends. Relations are an example of a persistent ambiguity of status. They are parts of pure experience, and yet common sense and radical empiricism have labeled them objective while rationalism and empiricism have called them subjective.

The homogeneity of the psychical and the physical in outer perception at the moment of direct sensation, which has just been pointed out, can also be predicated of imagination, memory, and the faculties of abstract representation. In analyzing the remembrance of the past there is no need to postulate its content as a tiny inner fact mirroring an absent reality which is projected into the distance; rather, the content presents itself from the first as the distant fact itself (*E.R.E.*, 264). In recalling the past a certain content is separated from all the physical intermediaries and joined to a new group of associates which enable it to re-enter mental life. As long as the phenomenon remains related to the physical intermediaries, it is classed as objective; when it becomes related to present associations, the same phenomenon is classed as thought. The reason inner representations are naively considered as being little spiritual copies of objects is that the vivacity of present objects contrasts so strongly with the weakness of our memories. But the fact is that the present object is constituted in the same way as the representation is, that is, both are sensations of the thing perceived. Even though a practical dualism is granted, "inasmuch as representations are distinguished from objects, stand in their stead and lead us to them, there is no reason to attribute to them an essential difference of nature" (*E.R.E.*, 265). Given the identity of being and perception within experience, the object and its representation are generally homogeneous.

Pure Experience as a Quasi-Chaos

Substitution is that aspect of experience whereby one part of experience, a representation, is said to stand for another, an object.

"Experience as a whole is a process in time," in which various terms supersede and follow one another through conjunctive or disjunctive transitions which are themselves features of experience and must be accounted as real as anything else (*E.R.E.*, 31). The nature of 'superseding' depends on which transition is being considered. In some cases one term follows another one which is simply dropped, while in other cases the subsequent terms carry on, enlarge, or bring to fulfillment, the earlier terms. These later representations fulfill the function of the earlier ones. Fulfilling a function in a world of pure experience, where transitions, departures, and arrivals are the only events, can be conceived of in only one way. "The only function that one experience can perform is to lead to another experience; and the only fulfillment we can speak of is the reaching of a certain experienced end" (*E.R.E.*, 32). Experiences, then, are for the sake of further experiences, in which they are said to terminate. When many experiences lead to the same end, they agree in function, even though the various paths traversed to get there may be very different. Indeed, the system of experiences, taken as presented at any given time, is a 'quasi-chaos' in that from any one term so many different paths may be taken which will yet lead to the same terminus. There can be no absolutely certain predictability as to which term will follow another in an experience, and this novelty of each occasion can be likened to a chaos, and yet many probable successions can be enumerated so that the chaos is not absolute but only relative. Even though either conceptual experience or sensible perception can be functionally substituted for each other, conceptualizations are highly advantageous paths to follow because of the extremely rapid transition which they yield, as well as their universal character and capacity for association in a great many systems.

Instead of the originary absolute chaos of consciousness which James postulated (with some reservations) in *The Principles of Psychology*, a quasi-chaos is proposed as best designating our experiences taken all together. Although we have been educated to notice and appreciate the continuities in our world of experience, there is vastly more discontinuity than we are commonly aware of. We are well aware of the continuous percepts which are our own body, the objective nucleus of each man's experience, and less aware of, though we may advert to them at any time, of the continuous percepts which give us our environing world, changing by gradual transition as we move about in it (*E.R.E.*, 33, n. 6). However, we are never present to the distant parts of the physical universe, which we are aware of through the intermediary of conceptual objects which are only rarely tied down to perceptual reality. Most of the physical universe does not impinge on our perceptual experience, but consists of partly shared and common and partly discrete objective nuclei of perceptions filled out by a vast number of conceptions which intersect those of other experients only at discontinuous perceptual points. Many experiences that make up what we consider to be the physical world are wholly subjective and non-substitutional and never end in the perceptual world. These networks of experiences which inter-relate with the objective nucleus of the shared physical world to make up each person's total experience of the world are not susceptible to organization into a coherent system of any kind. Inasmuch as these experiences are discontinuous, they are chaotic, but because, here and there, they do intersect with one another in the shared perceptual world, the chaos is not total, but only partial.

A quasi-chaos is not a patent absurdity, and to insist that either chaos or order must be asserted, but not both, or not some intermediate stage, is to fall into the trap of vicious intellectualism through arguing that order and chaos are contradictories, so that if one is true the other must be false. According to this logical objection, if the assertion is made that the primal given is chaotic, then it is false to claim that some aspect of the original given is not chaotic but is ordered. Hence, a quasi-chaos would be internally or inherently absurd. However, experience is far more complex and various than this single-edged logical analysis can exhibit. The logical interpretation of experience is only one way of taking reality, useful within its limitations, but powerless to encompass experience. The black and white rationality of traditional logic can only distort the flux of experience precisely as flux or process. What is true for the already structured propositional subject matter of logic has no necessary relation to what is true of the experience which antedates and is presupposed by that subject matter.

The insistence in chapter one that James could not hold both a chaotic and an ordered primal experience was based on his asserting two incompatible interpretations without realizing that they had to be reconciled in some way. To assert a quasi-chaos is not to claim that the original experience is ordered, when trying to account for the success of the natural sciences, and that it is chaotic when trying to account for the *a priori* nature of the pure sciences, as James did in the *Principles*, but to assert a primordial quasi-chaos in relation to all subsequent interpretations, including both the natural and the pure sciences. The notion of a quasi-chaos does not mean either a chaotic order or an orderly chaos, nor does it mean to baldly assert that order is present sometimes in pure experience and chaos is present at other times. Rather, a quasi-chaos is one in which order has not yet emerged as fully constituted, but nevertheless the continuity of the flux is real and provides the basis for many transitions. This notion is taken up again in more detail in chapter six.

PURE EXPERIENCE AS THE INSTANT FIELD OF THE PRESENT

Pure experience always means the instant field of the present. It is "plain unqualified actuality, a simple *that*, as yet undifferentiated into thing and thought, and only virtually classifiable as objective fact or as some one's opinion about fact" (*E.R.E.*, 36–37). Although this would seem to limit pure experience to perceptual activity, James says that conceptual fields as well as perceptual ones may be so designated. James's definition of ideas as the verbal equivalent of experience would bear out his assertion. Only a later experience, not pure experience taken in its immediacy, can retrospectively split the earlier one it supersedes into two parts, a content and a consciousness of that content. In the retrospective glance the immediate experience can be corrected or confirmed. The pure or present experience is not known to be true or false, although it may well be accepted as such; only a later judgment, separating content and consciousness, can pass judgment as to the validity of the content.

However, James repeatedly defines pure experience as "the immediate flux of life which furnishes the material to our later reflection with its conceptual categories" (*E.R.E.*, 46). Furthermore, "its purity is only a relative term, meaning the proportional amount of unverbalized sensation which it still embodies" (*E.R.E.*, 46). The instant field of the present, perceptual immediacy, is the most frequently and continuously affirmed explanation of pure experience given by James. Yet, he just as strongly insists that the primary attribute of pure experience is its neutrality—its indifference as to subject or object, perceptualization or conceptualization. Perhaps the apparent contradiction is due to the unreal stability inherent in analysis and conceptualization. In describing the hypothetical starting point of pure experience, James is forced to distinguish those primary parts of experience which have always been seen as constitutive of experience, i.e., percepts and concepts. Even though he was aware that pure experience is a metaphor or paradigm for a more primitive stage of experience before it is analyzed into later distinct elements, James continually emphasized perceptual experience as closer to original experience in its immediacy, unreflectiveness, and flux. Conse-

48

quently, he perhaps thought it necessary to include the field of conceptualization as also an example of pure experience in order to balance the emphasis on the perceptual features of experience. Although pure experience in its purity is neutral, James conceded that once we are able to talk about it at all, human experience is inextricably a mixture of perceptual and conceptual awareness. Hence, his recognition that pure experience is always a relative term, depending on the amount of reflection and verbalization involved.

This, of course, raises the larger question of the possibility and meaningfulness of such a thing as a non-experiential experience. If pure experience is never pure as experienced, then in what sense can it be spoken of meaningfully at all? I think that it can be as a limit concept which enables James to dethrone dualism as the primordial beginning of all experience. If experience is not necessarily split into subject and object, then many philosophical problems dissolve and new possibilities open up. By postulating a 'pure', i.e., neutral, experience as primordial, James challenges those who hold to the dualistic hypothesis to defend it on the same grounds, i.e., by how well that presupposition can handle the problems of experience and point the way to new possibilities.

A fundamental ontological dualism has been enshrined in the description of consciousness as an entity comprising half of every experience, the other half consisting in the content of consciousness. The persistent idea of a consciousness added to the content of things is due to an attempt to explain the undeniable fact that the content of experience, besides having its own existence, also interacts with and passes into other parts of experience in such a way as to leave an account of itself, so that the entire field of experience is transparent from one part to another (*E.R.E.*, 268). This bilaterality of the parts of experience, that they both are and are known, is misleadingly commonly explained as a fundamentally dualistic inner constitution belonging to every bit of experience. The function of being reported is seen as an ontological fact so that it is claimed to be, not an extrinsic relation, but a half part of the phenomenon itself. This temptingly plausible dualistic explanation can be overcome by hypothesizing that the primary reality is of a neutral nature and can be designated by an ambiguous name like 'phenomenon' or 'datum.' James says he prefers a plural formulation (although he does not use it again, as far as I am aware) and calls the primary reality pure experiences (*E.R.E.*, 268). These pure experiences are in continual transition, one with another, and enter into various relations, which are themselves essential parts of experience. These relations are just as much a conscious part of experience as are the terms of the relations. Consequently, fields of experience can be observed and classified. Because of the many, varied relations, the same experience can interact in different fields at the same time, being either physical or mental according to the context or setting.

CONCLUSION: THE STATUS OF RELATIONS IN
PURE EXPERIENCE AND IN THE CONTEXT OF EXPERIENCE

In conclusion, the assertions which opened this chapter, that relations are as directly experienced as are the terms of those relations, was substantiated by appealing to pure experience as the primordial reality underlying all subsequent experiences. James argued that the traditional thought-thing, subject-object dualism can be better explained in terms of secondary constructs by which mankind has gotten hold of and tried to make sense out of his world, rather than as an inevitable and necessary split of reality which man's experience both reflects and embodies. Pure experience as a hypothesis gives a better explanation of knowing, of subject and object, thought and thing, perception and conception, than does the alternate hypothesis of a primordial dualism. All of these contrasting terms do not stand for the constituents of various aspects of reality but are later additions which we have built into our experiences as a means of explaining them. Context, including the function of particular experiences, determines whether we shall call that experience subjective or objective; experiences do not occur already labeled. Perceptual experience, for example, is both physical and mental, and will be labeled as primarily concerning the one or the other, depending on which context of associates is emphasized. The world of concepts likewise gets sorted into a state of mind or field of objects according to the context of the various relations of the group of associates chosen as important in the given mental operation. The distinguishing characteristics of thoughts and things are more difficult to dichotomize than at first appears. Subject and object, thought and thing, are names for two groups into which we sort experiences according to the different type of interrelation into which they enter. Experiences are grouped with different sets of associates according to our practical or intellectual purposes.

The system of experiences is called a quasi-chaos in that the transitions and prospects of which it is composed cannot all be followed up in the subsequent experience; some will be preferred to others. Real transitions and prospects are given, but with no guarantee that one rather than another will prevail. Many discontinuities as well as continuities make up the networks of experiences that we call the physical world. Pure experience can be defined as the instant field of the present, the immediate flux of life before categorization. Its purity is a relative term, denoting the proportion of unverbalized absorption in the present sensation. Because consciousness as an experience both is and is known, it has usually been described as being dualistically constituted of two parts, a 'consciousness of' and a content. James substitutes the hypothesis of a primary reality of a neutral nature, designated 'phenomena' by some and 'pure experience' by him. These are actually pure experiences, since they are in continual transition and enter into various relations.

In explicating the hypothesis of pure experience a difficulty has gradually emerged, highlighted by the inclusion of perceptual and conceptual fields as examples of pure experiences. R. B. Perry has said that James's task is unfinished in that he raised difficulties and doubts without resolving them, particularly the question of the status of pure experience. "Is it a neutral stream of 'pure' experience, or is it the mental series, which constitutes the metaphysical reality?"[5] Sometimes James speaks as if it were exclusively one and sometimes the other. He does not resolve the ambiguity. We can make the most sense of the vacillation by considering the mental series, specifically consciousness, as the closest experienced reality to the paradigm of a neutral pure experience. Since pure experience is a limit concept, an explanatory hypothesis which can be postulated but not experienced as such, the stream of consciousness provides an experiential correlate which comes closest to pure experience and therefore is a useful model for explicating the more obscure hypothesis.

The explanation of pure experience as a limit concept, an experience which is by definition never immediately experienced, may be considered too paradoxical for some to assent to, especially since James himself has laid down the dictum that an empiricism is only radical insofar as it refuses to "admit into its construction any element that is not directly experienced" (E.R.E., 22). Perhaps a loophole can be found in this stricture by considering pure experience as on the cutting edge of ordinary experience. James does not say that pure experience is never experienced, but that it is never immediately experienced and communicated as such because as soon as anyone is conscious in a human sense, he already structures that consciousness according to conceptual and verbal categories. Pure experience is indeed the immediate flux of life which furnishes the raw material to later reflection, which is inextricably intertwined with conceptual categories.

However, "only new-born babes, or men in semi-coma from sleep, drugs, illnesses, or blows, may be assumed to have an experience pure in the literal sense of a *that* which is not yet any definite *what*, tho ready to be all sorts of whats . . ." (*E.R.E.*, 46). Since we cannot converse either with new-born babes or with semi-comatose persons, nor they with us, pure experience, as an experience, must remain a hypothesis, supported by experience and not contradicted by experience, to be sure, and yet not identical with ordinary experience.[6]

Although James also identifies pure experience as feeling or sensation, even feelings are interpreted as soon as they are experienced. The purity of pure experience is absolute only in incommunicable and therefore hypothetical cases; it is relative in ordinary experience, in which the unverbalized proportion of sensation is always overlaid with verbalized or conceptualized matrixes. It should also be recalled that for James the incommunicability of experience does not abrogate the experience (Cf., *Principles*, I, 251, "namelessness is compatible with experience"), but only demonstrates that conceptualization lags behind and never completely encompasses experience. I call such experiences 'hypothetical' to indicate that the experiences described can be pointed to, but not demonstrated, and so are open to alternate hypotheses or explanations on the rational level. James's terminology of "raw" and "cooked" experiences also seems invented to deal with this problem of uninterpreted or pure experience in relation to actual, lived experience.[7]

When once the hypothesis of a neutral pure experience, ever in flux, is broached, then descriptions can be found for experiences, especially fringe experiences, which come very close to being candidates for the original pure experience. This is no more proof for the experiential character of pure experience than the counter-argument that after postulating and elaborating a primordial dualism of mind and matter or consciousness and things or subject and object, it can be claimed that all actual experiences can be described dualistically and then using these supposed experiences of dualism as proof that dualism is directly experienced as the primordial given. Pure experience is such a fruitful notion because of its explanatory, not its descriptive, power. Although James emphasized the continuities of ordinary experience, he never denied that discontinuities are also experienced. He did object to taking the discontinuous experiences as the norm. By proposing a continuous, unbroken flux as the basic paradigm of experience, we will be induced in our ordinary, interpreted experience to take continuity and flux seriously and will, consequently, experience the transitions and not be fixated on the objectified world.

Relations are just as much part of direct particular experience as are things. Having just drawn the distinction between pure and 'impure' or ordinary experience, it is imperative to see how relations enter into both. Since experience in its pure state is neutral, consciousness and content, subject and object, thought and thing are later additions to an originally undivided 'that'. These dichotomies are functional attributes, discovered retrospectively according to which context is being considered. Relations in pure experience are quasi-chaotic in that they have not yet been hardened into specific identifiable relations which are attributable to a chosen context. In a world of pure experience, transitions, departures, and arrivals are the only events. Many transitions, both conjunctive and disjunctive, are going on, but once they are realized in a particular context as being physical or mental relations, they are no longer part of pure experience. Consequently, what is given in pure experience are multitudes of relations of transitions and tendency, not all of which will be realized in specific contexts. Incipient relations are present in the flux of pure experience, which is "full both of oneness and manyness, but in respects that don't appear; changing throughout, yet so confusedly that its phases interpenetrate and no points, either of distinction or of identity, can be caught" (*E.R.E.*, 46).

In ordinary experience relations become ideal or sensed according to the type of interaction involved in the given context. The context of associates which relations enter are qualified according to various functions and uses. A given perceptual experience will be counted either as a physical object, with all the concomitant physical relations, or as a subjective perception, with relations considered to be conscious and not physical, depending on which group of associates is taken up. The identical perceptual experience, a good model for pure experience, has many diverse relations which will be traced differently depending on which of them are followed up in ordinary or conceptualized experience—those of the field of consciousness or of physical history. As soon as the flux of pure experience is given it turns 'ordinary', and "tends to fill itself with emphases, and these salient parts become identified and fixed and abstracted; so that experience now flows as if shot through with adjectives and nouns and prepositions and conjunctions" (*E.R.E.*, 46). Ordinary experience is composed of explicit relations just as much as of explicit objects. Objects, after all, are identifiable matrixes of relations.

CHAPTER FOUR

THE EMPIRICIST OBJECTION TO EXPERIENCED
RELATIONS: JAMES AND HUME

Introduction

IT HAS BEEN claimed that James solved the problem of the reality
of relations. "Philosophically, this insight is of tremendous significance. It answers Hume's question squarely once and for all. . . ."[1]
It has also been countered that James could not even answer his own
questions.[2] One thing is certain: James was influenced by Hume and
developed his own philosophical outlook as a direct challenge to the
atomistic universe of the empiricists, represented pre-eminently by
Hume. As Perry pointed out: "James did not, as is commonly said,
begin with experimental psychology, but rather with British empiricism, which, in neglecting *felt relations*, also missed the essence of
things."[3] James was more vulnerable to attacks by the empiricists
than by the rationalists because he accepted the empiricist program
to a great extent. Indeed, he called his own philosophy "empirical,"
albeit radically so. But this very intimacy also spurred him to a more
detailed and cogent defense of his position against that aspect of empiricism with which he profoundly disagreed: the atomistic nature of
the world was rejected in favor of a continuous universe.

The recognized historical influence of Hume on James should be
mentioned. In the chapter on "The Believing Will" Julius Bixler
traces the age-old tension between the priority of the intellect and of
belief. He names the progenitors or, as he calls them, the "historical
antecedents," who can be seen as either influencing or anticipating

James's position. Those mentioned are Kant, Pascal, Renouvier; and among British thinkers, Thomas Reid and Sir William Hamilton are singled out for laying stress on the claims of belief as opposed to those of reason. Dean Mansel, Josiah Royce, and Friedrich Paulson are also mentioned as antedating James's position.[4] It is hard to see how Hume could be omitted from such a list. There is certainly enough of a relationship, indeed one sufficiently acknowledged by James, to warrant Hume a place among those whose thinking must be taken account of in assessing the historical antecedents of James. A more likely assessment of Hume's influence was given by Ettie Stettheimer. "Paulson, too seeks an historical place for James, and finds it in his own immediate neighborhood! In the introduction to the German translation of James' essays, he writes: 'Professor James belongs to a movement indicated by the names of Hume, Kant, Fichte and Carlyle'. . . ."[5] Ralph Barton Perry adds specific data in noting the importance Hume held for James: "James' serious study of Berkeley and Hume began, like that of Locke, about 1875, and culminated in 1883–1884 in the course on 'English Philosophy'."[6] John Dewey also testified to James's acknowledgment of his debt to Hume.[7]

In the following pages I will present first Hume's arguments against the reality of experienced relations, which is approached by way of an exposition on the role of belief in knowledge, then James's position. Next a comparison will be made of their common elements and an effort undertaken to determine if James accepted Hume's primary thrust in this matter. Their differences follow, mainly in order to determine if the differences arise from James correcting Hume's position or if James failed to really grapple with the issues involved. Lastly, a tentative answer will be given to the question of whether James's theory of experienced relations significantly went beyond Hume's explanation of belief or whether he only succeeded in showing how astutely Hume presented it.

HUME'S THEORY OF RELATIONS

The presentation of Hume's theory of relations is taken mainly from *A Treatise of Human Nature* supplemented by *An Inquiry Concerning Human Understanding*.[8] Hume reduces the connections or relations we observe among things to the operation of custom which induces us to think that we have a knowledge of relations when all we have is belief. He begins by defining belief, which does not consist in an idea or in a certain order of ideas but in the manner of their conception: "An opinion, therefore, or belief may be most accurately defin'd A LIVELY IDEA RELATED TO OR ASSOCIATED WITH A PRESENT OPINION" (*Treatise*, 96). In the *Enquiry* he reiterates the definition, which is held to throughout his treatment of belief: "I say, then, that belief is nothing but a more vivid, lively, forcible, firm, steady conception of an object, than what the imagination alone is ever able to attain" (*Enquiry*, 49). Since reason can never infer the existence of an object from that of another, the person proceeds by custom or the principle of association (*Treatise*, 97). The principles of association are reduced to three: resemblance, contiguity, and causation.

Hume says concerning resemblance: "I would willingly establish it as a general maxim in the science of human nature, that when any impression becomes present to us, it not only transports the mind to such ideas as are related to it, but likewise communicates to them a share of its force and vitality" (*Treatise*, 98). Although only the actual presence of an object lends a greater vivacity to its conception, "the thinking on any object readily transports the mind to what is contiguous" (*Treatise*, 100). Thirdly, causation will enliven any idea. By causation Hume means the constant conjunction of two objects so that the presence of one always leads us to expect the other. Since through experience a person has observed that certain objects or events follow one another and are constantly conjoined, he soon concludes that the one causes the other. But the conjunction may be merely arbitrary and casual since it is evident that no one knows by what 'powers' anything brings about another object or event, for such 'powers' are not visible to the senses. The principle which determines a person to continue thinking in terms of cause and effect is custom or habit (*Enquiry*, 42). Although an object was mentioned earlier, Hume soon makes it clear that it is not the object, but the present impression which is the cause of the idea. Since the phenomenon of belief is internal, unknown qualities or powers can have no hand in producing it.

No conclusion can be drawn from a single instance in isolation as to lead to belief. There must occur a number of instances, constantly conjoined with other impressions to produce belief. A mind can, however, from a single instance of cause or effect, infer the existence of its correlative when it is joined to a principle commonly experienced: "that like objects, placed in like circumstances, will always produce like effects" (*Treatise*, 105). All belief, then, is derived from custom. "Now as we call everything CUSTOM, which proceeds from a past repetition, without any new reasoning or conclusion, we may establish it as a certain truth, that all the belief, which follows upon any present impression, is derived solely from that origin" (*Treatise*, 103; cf.,

Inquiry, 43). Hume conveniently sums up what has been established so far:

1. 'Tis certain, we must have an idea of every matter of fact, which we believe.

2. 'Tis certain, that this idea arises only from a relation to a present impression.

3. 'Tis certain, that the belief super-adds nothing to the idea, but only changes our manner of conceiving it, and renders it more strong and lively.

4. The present conclusion concerning the influence of relation is the immediate consequence of all these steps; and every step appears to me sure and infallible (*Treatise*, 101).

Knowledge of both the continued existence of objects and of cause and effect operating in nature, is limited to belief because objects do not have any observable connection. It is only the principle of custom working upon imagination that leads us to infer from the appearance of one to the existence of another (*Treatise*, 103). The secret power operating in cause has nowhere been discovered because it is not present to the senses. About fifty pages later on Hume says: "The small success, which has been met with in all the attempts to fix this power, has at last oblig'd philosophers to conclude, that the ultimate force and efficacy of nature is perfectly unknown to us, and that 'tis in vain to search for it in all the known qualities of matter" (*Treatise*, 159).

There are two "natural beliefs" that Hume is concerned to account for: the continuing, independent existence of objects and the belief in causal dependence. Neither of these beliefs can be accounted for by reason alone. Objects, that is, the impressions of objects, are perceived only intermittently and no perception is identical to the one that went before it. Where, then, does the conviction arise that objects exist continuously and independently of any observer? It cannot be claimed that objects have any necessary existence because whatever exists may also not exist without entailing any absurdity. According to Hume, whatever is not known with certainty is not known at all, so that we do not *know* that objects exist independently of us, we only *assume* that it is so. But it is also true that "belief is *native* to sense perception; independently of any process of inference, it carries us to matter of fact and existence. . . ."[9]

Hume proceeds to account for this belief by the principles of association which are grounded in custom. "The *mental* transition is in no wise due to the objective nature of either the cause or the effect, but solely to their acquired connexion in the mind of the observer and the effects that follow thereupon."[10] The source of these inferences is to be found in us; from constant conjunction and the priority of one thing to another we come to infer that one thing is causing another. There is no way we can know that one thing is actually causing another because no such understanding of the nature of things is immediately given to our impressions. This is not to deny that things can influence one another independently of the mind, but there is no way that we could ascertain that this actually happens.

Hume's philosophy does not drive him to despair or to refuse to act because so much of our understanding of ourselves and the world is unreasonable. On the contrary, it is precisely because reason cannot be relied on in these essential areas of our conduct that nature removes us from the grip of skepticism by placing these 'matters of fact' under the sway of belief. Thus, although we might doubt external existences or causality, we must continue to act in their belief. Hume gives custom "equal weight and authority with reason" (*Enquiry*, 41). Although Hume carefully separated contingent truth from logical necessity, he did not do so at the expense of the former. Antony Flew quotes him as saying: "I never asserted so absurd a proposition as that anything might arise without a cause."[11]

Belief looms large on the horizon of Hume's philosophy because reason does not extend far enough. By pointing out the limits of reason Hume did not intend, like Locke, to limit our investigations to that sphere in which it could operate fully (it is much too narrow), but to point out that we operate on belief and passion as much in the area of knowledge as we do in the area of morals.

SIMILARITIES BETWEEN JAMES AND HUME

Nothing, perhaps, appears further from Hume's presentation of the need for belief to supply relations in the *Treatise* and the *Enquiry* than William James's opening to his essay, "The Will to Believe," in which he describes options as living or dead, forced or avoidable, momentous or trivial. However, a fuller exposition of James's theory of the roles of belief and experienced relations will lay a firm foundation for comparing and contrasting it with Hume's. With one exception, James's position will be presented from *The Will to Believe and Other Essays in Popular Philosophy* and *The Principles of Psychology*, since in these earlier works Hume's influence is more apparent. By way of contrast, James's more mature position in the *Essays in Radical Empiricism* will be brought in to determine how far he diverged from Hume.

James gives a rough definition of belief as the mental state of cognizing reality. Whenever he uses 'belief' in *The Principles of Psychology* he means by it all degrees of assurance, from the most tentative to the highest possible certainty and conviction (*Principles*, II, 283). Compare James's admission: "Belief, the sense of reality, feels like itself—that is about as much as we can say," (*Principles*, II, 286) with Hume's "I confess, that it is impossible perfectly to explain this feeling or manner of conception" (*Enquiry*, 49). James points out the relation of reality to our emotional and active life. He explicitly credits Hume with first recognizing the relationship. "*In this sense, whatever excites and stimulates our interest is real*: whenever an object so appeals to us that we turn to it, accept it, fill our mind with it, or practically take account of it, so far it is real for us, and we believe it. . . . Hume's account of the matter was then essentially correct, when he said that belief in anything was simply the having the idea of it in a lively and active manner" (*Principles*, II, 295). He then quotes the *Treatise*, bk. 1, pt. iii, sec. 7. James's list of six ways objects are maintained in belief can be compared with Hume's position.[12]

James also remarks that belief in matters of fact is not under our will. We can no more believe that something is present to our perception which is not, than we can ignore a present impression. "We can *say* any of these things, but we are absolutely impotent to believe them, and of just such things is the whole fabric of the truths that we do believe in made up,—matters of fact, immediate or remote, as Hume said, and relations between ideas, which are either there or not there for us if we see them so, and which if not there cannot be put there by any action of our own" (*W.B.*, 5).

Custom and habit are as intrinsic to belief for James as they are for Hume. A great deal of our thinking is compounded of habits which have been impressed on us from without. The degree to which our thoughts cohere is one with the causes and objects of our thought (*Principles*, II, 632). In another place James remarks that mere familiarity is enough to produce a feeling of rationality and that the empiricists have been so struck by this fact that they have defined rationality as nothing more than the feeling of familiarity. Repeatedly seeing the same phenomena juxtaposed in the same way leads to a conviction of their connection that is every bit as certain as the theoretical insight into their coherence. Custom, which allows us to explain a thing by recalling its antecedents and to know it by being able to predict its consequents, is thus the source for the rationality we attribute to the knowing process (*W.B.*, 77). James again speaks about custom and belief in very Humean words, which deserve to be quoted because of their echoes of Hume's vocabulary as well as point of view:

> To uniform outer coexistences and sequences correspond constant conjunctions of ideas, to fortuitous coexistences and sequences casual conjunctions of ideas. We are sure that fire will burn and water wet us, less sure that thunder will come after lightning, not at all sure whether a strange dog will bark at us or let us go by. In these ways experience moulds us every hour, and makes of our minds a mirror of the time- and space-connections between the things and the world. The principle of habit within us so *fixes* the copy at last that we find it difficult even to imagine how the outward order could possibly be different from what it is, and we continually divine from the present what the future is to be. (*Principles*, II, 619)

In his earlier writings James also takes Hume's position in regard to causality as a human construct to account for constant conjunction. James holds that the principle of causality is only a postulate, an empty name which stands in for the reality we hope one day to discover. It is a demand that the sequence of events which we experience will some day show a deeper cohesion than the merely arbitrary juxtaposition we are familiar with (*W.B.*, 147). He again acknowledges his debt to Hume: "Hume's account of causation is a good illustration of the way in which empiricism may use the principle of totality. We call something a cause; but we at the same time deny its effect to be in any way contained in or substantially identical with it. We thus cannot tell what its causality amounts to until its effect has actually supervened" (*W.B.*, 147). However, two lines later he radically disassociates himself from full agreement with Hume by asserting that we experience all the relations of a thing if we experience it at all. If we know things as they exist, they must be known in all the relations which appear as part of them and this in a single fact of consciousness. To know something means to know a congery of experienced relations. The unity of apprehension is constituted by the "relation yielding matrix" through which we experience the world, e.g., time, space, and the mind of the knower. In the *Essays in Radical Empiricism*, written later, James argues even more explicity for the reality of the phenomena of causality and shows the meaninglessness of looking for a hidden metaphysical principle behind what we experience. "I conclude then that real effectual causation as an ultimate nature, as a 'category,' if you like, of reality, is *just what we feel it to be*, just that kind of conjunction which our own activity-series reveal" (*E.R.E.*, 93).

DIFFERENCES

James speaks of a harmony between our powers of knowing and reality. But he also departs from what was heretofore recognized as what was given in perception and what was inferred. He insists that both conjunctions and disjunctions are equally given in experience. At the same time, he also insists on the paradox, already raised in the first chapter of this study, between fragmentary impressions being given and a ordered outlook on life resulting: "What we experience, what comes before us, is a chaos of fragmentary impressions interrupting each other, what we *think* is an abstract system of hypothetical data and laws" (*Principles*, II, 634). He also points out that the harmony has to be actively sought in order to be found. Belief enters in, not merely in enlivening an idea, but as an agent bringing about what it expects to find. This harmony of man and nature is created as much as it is found. The principle of the uniformity of nature, far from being given in appearance, has to be sought despite contrary evidence. That we are convinced that it is true is due more to our propensity to believe than to any intellectual assent to a demonstration. Stability also characterizes belief. The idea fills the mind to the exclusion of contradictory ideas. Since this is true, the opposite of belief is not disbelief but doubt. The psychological states of doubt and inquiry, the real opposites of belief, are characterized by an unrest in the content of the mind, and this emotion, like the emotion of belief, is perfectly distinct, although not describable in words (*Principles*, II, 636-637; 284).

Already in *The Principles of Psychology* James explained that ideas and sensations do not enter consciousness piecemeal but are part of a stream of consciousness and that consciousness includes the apprehension of relations as well as elements. When he later transformed the paradigm of the stream of consciousness into that of pure experience, he called his philosophical outlook "radical empiricism," thereby calling attention to both the similarity of his view with that of his predecessors and his specific differentiating principle. He accepts the basic approach of empiricism, which starts with the individual elements of consciousness and looks upon the universal as an abstraction and which begins with the parts as given and makes of the whole a second order reality (*E.R.E.*, 22). But connections are as much part of the primary data of consciousness as are specific ideas; both find their origins in impressions. James's empiricism is unique and called radical because it refuses both to recognize anything that is not directly experienced and to ignore anything that is directly experienced, and therefore accepts the givenness of relations since the relations that connect experiences are experienced relations and must be accounted as real as anything else in the system (*E.R.E.*, 22).

FURTHER SIMILARITIES

For James, as for Hume, belief is the kernel of all judgment of matters of fact. James also considers it as the same psychical attitude of will because of his understanding of the selectivity of the mind among a continuing stream of consciousness out of which the person selects those substantive states attended to. There are three concentric areas of knowledge. First is the nucleus of immediate experience where an organism interacts with others in its environment. Next is the area of theoretic judgment in which belief is partially supported by notions of consistency, resemblance, and other judgments of verifiability. Third, lies the area of faith which is supported only partially or more often, negatively, by reason. That is, it is not contradictory that such religious beliefs are the ultimate explanation of nature, although it can never be demonstrated that they actually are valid.[13] For James the quality of life which results from such beliefs is their only and sufficient verification.

The ultimate reality is the sense of our own lives which is always present to us and which other objects must share to some degree in order to be believed in by us. Therefore, primacy must be given to objects of sensation which compel us by their vividness and liveliness and to concepts insofar as they share immediacy by association with these primary data. These concepts must be found to originate in direct impressions or to terminate in action or emotion.[14] "But now we are met by questions of detail. What does this stirring, this exciting power, this interest consist in, which some objects have: which are those 'intimate relations' with our life which give reality? And what things stand in these relations immediately, and what others are so closely connected with the former that (in Hume's language) we 'carry our disposition' also on to them?" (*Principles*, II, 299). Shortly after James asks these questions, which are grounded in a Humean interpretation of belief, he answers that any relation to our mind at all, when no stronger relation attracts us, is enough to reify an object.

Whatever we turn our mind to with dominant attention, to the exclusion of anything else, is believed by us in some degree. Those which command our attention with greater force are more fully believed than those which are fleeting and fragmentary. Thus, while we give some credence to dreams while we are actually having them, on awaking, the greater vivacity of the everyday impressions speedily erases the dream impressions.

James's inheritance from Hume of the hypothetical and non-demonstrable basis of most judgments concerning everyday life influenced him to regard events as chaotic so that rationality must be added to experience by us. "He came very near to accepting the disconnected flux of events which Hume bequeathed to his successors; his quotations show that he fully appreciated the skill with which Hume had exposed the futility of the explanations which explained nothing."[15] However, the general chaos espoused in *The Principles of Psychology* was later rejected by James, as well as the too limited understanding of rationality as identical with abstract conceptualization. James rejected the mind as a mere passive entity receiving im-impressions; for him we are always agents, actively soliciting by our interest that to which we will be attentive. With the myriad sense impressions constantly bombarding our consciousness, we reject as much or more than we are attentive to. But it is equally true that experience comes pregnant with associations and tendencies which can be ignored only at our own risk.

It would be distortive to explain James's attitude toward belief without referring to Hume. Even if a person were so inclined, he would have to ignore large segments of James's exposition where Hume is explicitly mentioned. Some of the more striking areas of agreement will be explored further to see if the similarity is more than just surface correspondence. Although James more frequently mentions Hume when he wants to depart from his positions, this compulsion to answer Hume's supposed objections has a formative influence on the shape James's exposition of belief and experienced relations takes.

James shares with Hume what is understood as the empiricist theory of knowledge. As was indicated earlier, this means that experience cannot be anticipated by logical proofs. Whatever exists may also cease to exist without entailing any contradiction. Therefore, any particular existence can never be demonstrated. Furthermore, Hume held that since we do not know 'the inmost nature' of anything, we must look for the origin of such beliefs as continued, independent existence and efficacious cause and effect relationships elsewhere than in the immediate sense data and finds this source in the principles of association and custom. James, however, disagrees with this analysis. He sees no necessity for trying to imagine a realm of essences behind sense data, or to draw false conclusions from their absence, since everything needed to explain cause and effect, as well as the other relations, is given in ordinary experience. In a century labeled by historians as "The Age of Reason" Hume exposed the limitations of formal reasoning and proved that all judgments about matters of fact are beliefs only and not rational demonstrations. Belief is a central constituent of the philosophies of both Hume and James: "The real heart of Hume is his belief in belief. He carefully established a position: since we cannot know, cannot prove in the strict sense, we must believe. . . ."[16] The centrality of belief to James's writing is also evident to anyone with even a fleeting acquaintance with him, but is developed as an aspect of human rationality and not as a weak substitute for rational demonstration.

James and Hume did share a common attitude toward the cosmos. The perfect order and regularity ascribed to the universe is due more to man's propensity to think it so, than it is to any objective evidence. The irregularity of nature is as much a datum of experience as is any order and harmony. James expresses this insight as the presence of novelty in experience. He credits empirical skepticism with keeping men aware of the merely assumed nature of a 'block universe' which is conceived of as totally intelligible. This over-confident pride in the optimistic outcome of events has led empiricists to emphasize their skepticism, as when they remind us of the many real possibilities, alien to our accepted pictures of the universe, which may nonetheless come about and eclipse any system we have established (*W. B.*, 81).

The vividness of ideas as an essential constituent of belief has already been noted as a common ground between James and Hume. Although James agreed with Hume that in sensation liveliness of perception could neither be solicited nor ignored, he gave a person a much greater latitude in determining just which percepts will occupy the center of consciousness and which will be relegated to the fringe of consciousness. It is doubtful, though, whether vividness of perception is sufficient to account for belief. If the only difference between a phantasy and a perception is the liveliness of the perception, what about the person with an unusually vivid imagination? If vividness were the only criterion, the person would have no way of separating his phantasy from his percept; how could he ever know that his more vivid phantasy has no objective existence? Yet people with lively imaginations do manage to distinguish between the two.[17]

JAMES'S RADICAL DISASSOCIATION FROM HUME

Because James has so closely followed Hume's lead in explaining belief, their differences are the more highlighted. In the following exposition I will attempt to show that James's deviations from Hume's position are deliberate changes which improve upon and go beyond Hume's philosophy, and that James did not misconstrue the thrust of Hume's arguments and so differ from him by default. It seems that the source for James's differences with Hume are found in elements of his philosophy which are no less integral to his philosophical position than is the influence of Hume. Therefore, these are no fortuitous divergencies but point up fundamental orientations in both philosophers.

As has already been indicated, the major difference between Hume and James lies in their differing approaches to relations. A juxtaposition of their viewpoints in this regard should serve to point out the irreconcilability of their respective stands on this issue. According to Hume:

> Reason can never show us the connexion of one object with another, tho' aided by experience, and the observation of their constant conjunction in all past instances. . . . Had ideas no more union in the fancy than objects seem to have to the understanding, we cou'd never draw any inference from causes to effects, nor repose belief in any matter of fact. (*Treatise*, 92)

However, Hume does not repose in a grossly disconnected world, but proceeds to explain where the apprehension of relations is to be found.

> We have no other notion of cause and effect, but that of certain objects, which have been *always conjoin'd* together, and which in all past instances have been found to be inseparable. We cannot penetrate into the reason of the conjunction. We only observe the thing itself, and always find that from the constant conjunction the objects acquire an union in the imagination. (*Treatise*, 92)

After James acknowledged that he is basically following a "Humean type of empiricism," which begins with the parts and makes of the whole a being of the second order, he points out their divergency.

> *The relations that connect experiences must themselves be experienced relations, and any kind of relation experienced must be accounted as*

'real' as anything else in the system. Elements may indeed be redistributed, the original placing of things getting corrected, but a real place must be found for every kind of thing experienced, whether term or relation, in the final philosophic arrangement. (*E.R.E.*, 22)

James agrees with Hume that we must build a satisfactory theory of knowledge out of the smallest bits of data present to our consciousness. For Hume consciousness consists of discrete "particals" of impressions, sensations, and ideas, and immediate experience is of one or other of these taken separately. Not so for James. His primary given is pure experience, called at various times, a stream of consciousness or a sensible flux out of which separate bits are picked for the sake of analysis. Although both continuities and discontinuities are equally given in experience, in the past only the discontinuities were taken as immediately given, and it was assumed that the continuity of relations was supplied by the mind in its operations of knowledge. James reasons that since our relations are immediately given, they must be considered as much a primary datum as any other that empiricists appeal to. He says that we have as much a feeling for 'and' and 'if' as we do for 'blue' and 'cold'.

Now Hume also said that there may be relations in nature corresponding to causality but that if there are, we could never know it because we have no faculty to grasp such a relationship.[18] We can, by attending to the operations of our own minds, infer from contiguity, resemblance, and constant conjunction to the probability of cause and effect, but we can never prove it. To this James answers that we do have natural faculties that can apprehend such a relationship. "If we survey the field of history and ask what feature all great periods of revival, of expansion of the human mind, display in common, we shall find, I think, simply this: that each and all of them have said to the human being, 'The inmost nature of reality is congenial to *powers* which you possess' " (*Principles*, II, 314). Both positions depend on what is immediately present to consciousness. James, for his part, accuses Hume of psychological atomism: "The traditional psychology talks like one who should say a river consists of nothing but pailsful, spoonsful, quartpotsful, barrelsful and other moulded forms of water" (*Principles*, I, 155). James felt he was remedying Hume's blindness to connections by emphasizing the continuous flow of our experiences. Still, Hume would probably answer: "As an agent, I am quite satisfied in the point [that my practice refutes my doubts]; but as a philosopher, who has some shade of curiosity, I will not say skepticism, I want to learn the foundation of this inference" (*Enquiry*, 35).

To frame an answer to Hume it will first be necessary to touch on his explanation of induction. Although Hume formulated the problem of induction, he also admits that there are some causes of which the effects have always been seen to follow. Even though he gives a logically satisfying answer as to why future events do not necessarily have to continue to follow the same cause and effect pattern, he does not give any satisfactory reason why in some instances they do in fact follow regularly (*Enquiry*, 57). One of the motives for Hume's philosophy was to account for the probable nature of our reasoning about matters of fact. He says that judging from present occurences, we have no right (that is, reasonable basis) for doing so. Since we have no absolute knowledge of anything, except mathematical conclusions which are necessarily so, we have no reasonable knowledge at all, but only belief. But it can be asked of Hume, why, to be reasonable, does something have to be absolutely predictable? Man's power to reason extends to more realms than logic. Hume mentions two categories of causes: those which have admitted of no exception and those which have been more uncertain. His explanation of cause hinges on the unpredictability of any cause in the absolute sense. In other words, he has chosen to stress those causes which have proven unpredictable in the past and to ignore those which have never failed. He can only impugn the actuality of these never-failing causes and effects by saying that some time in the future they *may* not continue to do so.

This argument weighs so heavily with Hume because it can be contrasted with the absolute predictability of the world of mathematics. It is not inherently contradictory that a certain effect does not proceed from a given cause but that two plus two ever equal anything but four *is* inherently contradictory. Since matters of fact obviously differ from purely formal relations, why do both have to fulfill the same conditions (e.g., a proposition of which the contradictory is not absurd) in order to be reasonable? Is it not *un*reasonable to expect both to conform to the same rules in the same way? Even those causes and effects which have admitted of no exception do not fulfill the requirements of Hume's proposition; but do matters of fact have to fit that Procrustean bed in order to be accepted as reasonable and not only believable?

This same matter is taken up by H. H. Price in "The Permanent Significance of Hume's Philosophy."[19] The crux of the matter lies in what a person considers reasonable. The definition of reasonable which prevailed in Hume's time (and for many today) was that "a process of thought is reasonable if it exemplifies the principles of formal or deductive inference, laid down in Formal Logic. . . ."[20] Now if it is a person's conviction that all valid inference ought to be deductive, Hume is right, and the most to be hoped for is belief. But Price also points out that the "capacity to learn the lessons of experience, to frame one's generalizations (and consequently one's predictions and retrodictions) in accordance with one's whims and fancies, hopes and fears, suppressed desires and the like—this capacity is most certainly an essential element in the make-up of a 'reasonable' man, as common sense conceives of him."[21]

James's contribution fits in precisely here; he expands the province of rationality. His insistence that relations are experienced and that man possesses the power to apprehend those relations would attack the skeptical argument of the irrationality of causal relations. How do we then account for James's statements, already quoted, in which he reiterates, with approval, Hume's insistence that custom alone leads us to believe in causal connections? Perhaps part of the answer lies in the dates of these earlier references. *The Principles of Psychology* was first published in 1890, the "Will to Believe" was delivered as a lecture in 1896, *The Will to Believe and Other Essays* was first published in 1897. But the *Essays in Radical Empiricism* was published only posthumously in 1912. The position known as radical empiricism was anticipated in a paper called "Does 'Consciousness' Exist?" delivered in 1904.[22] In this essay the traditional substantive view of consciousness is rejected in favor of the view that consciousness is relational.[23] Radical empiricism is applied to the theory of knowledge the same year in "A World of Pure Experience."[24] With the thesis of pure experience James was able to bridge the gap between experienced relations and *a priori* knowledge without doing violence to the tentative character of experience and the creative agent.

Is this really so different from Hume's position as it seems? Hume also speaks of a pre-established harmony between nature and our ideas. "Here, then, is a kind of pre-established harmony between the course of nature and the succession of our ideas; and though the powers and forces, by which the former is governed, be wholly unknown to us; yet our thoughts and conceptions have still, we find, gone on in the same train with the other works of nature. Custom is that principle, by which this correspondence has been effected . . ." (*Enquiry*, 54–55). James, however, rejects the appeal to the unknown powers of nature and provides an explanation of why our ideas harmonize with the course of nature. The reason is that nature as we experience it has already been affected by the interaction. Pure nature or pure experience exhibits tendencies, conjunctions and disjunctions, which we bring to fulfillment through our intervention, whether that intervention brings about specific objects and relations through a context of action or the direction provided by a scientific or other theory or, even, by custom or common sense.

Within the doctrine of pure experience, James's demonstration of observable relations would give a reasoned basis for the pre-established harmony, and man's powers being congenial to the nature of reality would replace custom as an explanatory principle. It could still be charged that these two assertions of James have to be taken on faith, or at any rate cannot be demonstrated. And according to demonstration in the strict sense, this charge would hold. However, belief in our understanding of nature through custom, and belief in the immediate apprehension of relations are on an equal footing so far as beliefs go, and each person would have to decide for himself which of the two better represents experience as we know it. However, James's theories of pure experience and selective activity, which assert that tendencies, connections, and disconnections, exist before they are ever structured by a subsequent act of selection arising from a context, seem more successful in handling both ordinary experience and the problems of philosophy.

James pointed out another crucial difference between himself and Hume. Hume's propensity to cut up the flux of consciousness into unchangeable bits or concepts has already been mentioned. This means that Hume has to look to the origins of his concepts in order to verify them, since concepts are retrospective, coming after the fact. James, seeking to identify the inner relations of experienced nature, hopes to gain some measure of control over the future.[25] This difference between James and his predecessors in Britain has been expressed as the temporal reference of ideas and beliefs. Whereas empiricists had emphasized the reference to the past, James emphasizes the reference to the future. An idea is justified by what it leads to or allows to happen, and not by its origin.

This brings in the aspect of agency, which plays a large part in James's philosophy. It is only as agents that we become concerned with reliability. For James we *know* in order to *do*. Hume was careful to safeguard the rights of the agent by putting those most active aspects of life under a customary approach which cannot be ignored by the person or refuted by skepticism. However, it is questionable whether by narrowly prescribing the limits of reason, he did not thereby seriously restrict the interplay of reason and matters of fact which occupy so large a part of our day.

The inert and detached world of pure technical logic . . . has apparent-ly no place for any notion of contingent reliability, as opposed to the total but empty assurance of logical necessity. Nor does it have room for the distinction, which is so important in the testing of claims to possess that contingent reliability, between merely observational and active experimental evidence. We may thank Hume for providing us in his negative analysis with an instrument which can take the mystery out of agency.[26]

But at the same time we are not disinterested spectators in the play of life. While Hume emphasized the importance of agency by removing it from the sphere of critical discussion, James integrated the agent within the whole process of knowing and being by showing that without selective interest percepts cannot even be discriminated out of the stream of consciousness and without the imposition of a context on pure experience the human life-world would neither exist nor be explainable. Logical necessity is but one of the ways we organize the world and it is not prescriptive for other points of view.

CONCLUSION

Many of James's premises originated in the British Empiricist tradition. His explanations of belief, exclusive of his doctrine of relations, is almost totally Humean. However, James's development of the thesis of directly apprehended relations profoundly shifts the emphasis on the role of belief and undercuts whatever similarities exist between his theory of belief and Hume's. According to John J. McDermott, "This insight of the experiencing of 'transitive relationships' will ultimately force James to hold a different view of the source of intelligibility and will render the role of logical relations as external and derivative."[27] Although there is certainly a continuity of interest in both men concerning the problem of belief, their differences are more significant. Both gave the greater weight to belief over reason in the everyday affairs of life, whether great or small, but James achieved his greatest insights in this matter precisely from wrestling with Humean positions. James's doctrines of experienced relations and powers congenial to perceiving them are answers to Hume's atomistic data of perception and inability to find an intrinsic source for the belief in causality. He succeeded in incorporating the best of the Humean insights, while going beyond his shortcomings, and satisfactorily answered Hume's challenge through demonstrating the intelligibility native to experience.

70

CHAPTER FIVE

CONJUNCTIVE RELATIONS AND THE RATIONALIST OBJECTION TO EXPERIENCED RELATIONS: JAMES AND BRADLEY

INTRODUCTION

THE INTERWEAVING of the claim that relations are a matter of direct particular experience with the hypothesis of pure experience was demonstrated in chapter three. As was noted, James's radical empiricism is a manifesto that his way of philosophizing neither admits into its construction any element not directly experienced nor excludes any element that is so experienced. Radical empiricism is, further, a statement of the fact that the relations that connect experiences are themselves experienced and that previous philosophies have ignored or denied the fact that relations are as much matters of direct particular experience as are things. Both ordinary empiricism and rationalism deny the reality of relations in experience. Ordinary empiricism, represented by Berkeley, Hume, and Mill, have denied that both conjunctive and disjunctive relations are fully co-ordinate parts of experience and have insisted on the disjunctions at the expense of the connectedness of things (*E.R.E.*, 23). The empirical position, with Hume as its most influential originator, was presented in some detail in chapter four. Rationalism, represented by Hegel, Herbart, and Bradley, also deny that relations are part of experiential reality and claim that not one of the conjunctive relations between things is rationally possible (*E.R.E.*, 52). Consequently, they insist that non-experiential

principles or agents must be brought in to unify an otherwise disconnected world of experience. Radical empiricism opposes both ordinary
empiricism and rationalism by doing full justice to conjunctive relations. In this chapter James's arguments in favor of conjunctive relations will be set out in more detail than heretofore. This will be
followed by his arguments against the rationalist position as exemplified in his polemics against Bradley.

EXTERNAL AND INTERNAL RELATIONS

According to James, relations, in a universe of discourse, range from
external to intimate.[1] The most external relation that terms can have,
whether in a mental or physical series, is "merely to be 'with' one
another"; no consequences follow from the mere conjunction of one
term with another. The most 'intimate' relation is that "between terms
that form states of mind, and are immediately conscious of continuing each other" (*E.R.E.*, 23). This relation almost disappears in identity, with no demarcation point for the beginning of one term and the
end of another, which seem to compenetrate each other's being. Compared to this most intimate relation of consciousness, the organization
of the self as a self-contained system constituted by memory, purposes,
and expectations, seems merely incidental. The scale of relations, in
the order of ascendency from external to intimate, are: simultaneity,
time-interval, space-adjacency, distance, similarity and difference, and
relations of activity. Many inferences already become possible with
similarity and difference, whereas the causal order is tied to the relations of activity, involving as they do, change, tendency and resistance.

The criterion for calling a relation more or less external or internal seems to be the inevitability and predictability or necessity of consequences in an internal relation as opposed to the fortuitousness,
unpredictability, or even lack of consequences in an external relation.
James also hints that the multiplicity of consequences is also a criterion. Perhaps he means that the more that can be predicted with
certainty from a given relation the more intimate it is. To be 'with'
one another is a prime example of an extrinsic relation in that even
though something may follow from the fact that one term is with another term, there is no necessity that anything in particular must follow
from the relation of 'withness', such that from the inspection of the
relationship alone, one could say that X must follow, given any term
'with' another term. In contrast, the terms that form states of mind
necessarily follow one another and are conscious of each other, be-

72

cause states of mind are continuous or else they are not states of mind. James would not say that the relationship is necessary because of stipulation or definition, but that the definition follows from an inspection of actual states of mind.

James was aware that philosophy recapitulates grammar for some time before Wittgenstein made this insight the cornerstone of his *Investigations.*[2] Much of what passed as traditional philosophical relations are in reality thinly disguised grammatical particles. The various grammatical particle-relations, for instance, can also be arranged in an ascending order from external to intimate: "with, near, next, like, from, towards, against, because, for, through, my" (*E.R.E.*, 24). A new criterion is added with this order, that of inclusiveness. Whatever relations are subsumed under other relations are more extrinsic than the ones they are subsumed under. The more intimate the relation, the more relations are included with it. That is, those relations which must necessarily be presupposed in order to account for a relation, are 'inferior' to the relation with the greater extension. The concept of withness does not presuppose any other relation, thus it is an extrinsic relation. However, the concept of nextness presupposes or includes the concept of withness. Therefore, it is less extrinsic and more intimate than withness. The concept of likeness presupposes those of withness and of nextness, but adds a further dimension to them and so is more intimate than they. No level of relation demands the next higher level, but each presupposes the one below it. Each relation reveals a different level of unity and is thus far its own universe. The concept 'my' symbolizes the universe of human experience which includes all the other levels. It should be noted that James does not use the word, "concept," in this context, but speaks of "grammatical particles," "conjunctive relation," and "universe." Thus, from the perspective of language, grammatical particles are at issue, from the perspective of experience, conjunctive relations are at issue.

CONSCIOUS TRANSITION AS A CONJUNCTIVE RELATION

One particular conjunctive relation which has priority over the others both temporally and in importance, is the "co-conscious transition." The co-conscious transition signifies that one experience passes into another immediately, with no intervening hiatus, when both belong to the same self (*E.R.E.*, 25). This happens to those experiences I call mine, as well as to those experiences you call yours, but never to yours and mine together. In fact, mine are distinguished from yours and from everyone else's by this very continuity. In one's personal history, subject, object, interest, and purpose follow one another or may follow one another continuously. This continuous transition in one's personal history is a process of change in time, and this change itself is immediately experienced. Radical empiricism starts with the fact of the continuous transition as one sort of conjunctive relation which is immediately experienced, "for this is the strategic point, the position through which, if a hole be made, all the corruptions of dialectics and all the metaphysical fictions pour into our philosophy" (*E.R.E.*, 25). This fact must be taken at face value, if it is to be taken at all, for it grounds all the postulates and conclusions of radical empiricism and pragmatism. As a primordial fact it is immediately given, or in James's terminology, something to be taken just as we feel it. Any descriptions of it are secondary and have meaning only insofar as they point to the original feeling or immediate experience.

The continuous passage by which one moment of personal experience inconspicuously merges into another is felt before it is ever conceptualized. This experience of continuity is just as definite as the experience of discontinuity which is felt in adverting to someone else's experience. A positive break can be duly noted in passing from one's own immediate awareness to thinking about someone else's. In the latter case something must be cognized, a leap made to another state of affairs in contrast to the more familiar lived experiences of one's personal history. Even when the functions of the two experiences are the same, when the same objects are known and the same purposes followed by both, they are not present in the same way as part of one's own experience and as what one takes to be part of someone else's experience. A definite break is felt in passing from one's own felt experiences to an awareness of someone else's. The sameness of objects in both cases is not arrived at in the same way. In one's own case, the identity of object and interest through successive passing moments continues without break within a lived experience, while the acknowledgement that someone else is aware of the same object involves a conscious decision, which does not preclude elements of doubt and qualification.

The source for the ideas of continuity and sameness can be found in the way perception operates. The continuous transition of one moment or Gestalt in one's personal experience into the next moment or Gestalt, without break, is the experiential basis, the original conjunctive relation that 'grounds' the concepts of continuity and conjunctive relation. Agreeing with Hume that the meaning of an idea is ultimately reducible to the sense experience which is its original, James defends his claim that the discreteness of distinct perceptions, insofar as they

are derivable experientially, are a later refinement of a more fundamental experience of continuity. This experience of one's own continuity, the actual experience which the word 'continuity' stands for,
is all that is finally meant by continuity and sameness (*E.R.E.*, 26).
Both empiricists and rationalists deny the immediacy of continuity,
since everything is either the same or different. If they are the same,
then there are not two things but one identical thing and therefore
no continuity between things; if they are different, then they must be
joined by a third thing, which in turn must be joined, and so on *ad
infinitum*. Such a multiplicity of discrete things could never be taken
as a transition as Plato already demonstrated (e.g., *Parmenides*, 128 E
ff. and *Sophist*, 251 C ff.). For the empiricists the original perceptions
are of singulars, which they leave disjointed, while for the rationalists,
the explanation of perception demands an appeal to transcendental
principles of unity, which must be added to 'mere' experience in order
to make it intelligible.

James counters this appeal to a disjointed universe with the assertion that continuity and discontinuity are both given in experience,
and that it is as capricious to exclude the one as the other in our
later reflection on the given phenomena (*E.R.E.*, 26–27). Conjunctions
and separations are equally real, being co-ordinate phenomena given
in experience. If it is found necessary to appeal to transcendental
principles to join what has first been separated out of continuously
joined experiences, it must equally be necessary to appeal to similar
principles to account for the discontinuity of what is originally continuous. Conversely, if it is not necessary to assume such principles
in the one case, it should not be necessary to assume them in the
other.

JAMES AND BRADLEY

While it can be said that James was both a pupil and a critic of
Hume, he was only a critic of F. H. Bradley. Although James readily
sympathized with Bradley when he found points on which they could
agree, he did not develop his own philosophy by first building on and
then opposing Bradley. In fact, James found such polemic writing as
he engaged in with Bradley extremely odious, justified only by the
fact that the popularity of absolutism, of which Bradley was one of the
prime exponents, demanded refutation if James's own position was to
be taken seriously. Consequently, Bradley's position will be explicated
from James's point of view, since Bradley's philosophy is important
for an understanding of James's theory of relations only insofar as it

stood as a foil which enabled James to clarify some aspects of his own theory of relations and to answer some of the most prominent objections put forward by an influential opposing school of thought.

The main point of contention between James and Bradley involved the affirmation or denial of internal or intrinsic relations and extrinsic relations. A commentator on Bradley puts the disagreement succinctly:

> Accordingly, Bradley's denial of external relations, his insistence that, if we are to choose between classifying relations as external or internal, then indubitably they must all be regarded as internal—the 'apparent externality' (A.R., p. 517) of some relations, like the apparent contingency of some judgments, being merely the projection of our ignorance upon the world—is certainly the most unambiguous argument he urged, the directest blow he struck, against Pluralism and in favour of Monism.[3]

This is immediately followed by an admission that "like a great deal of Bradley's thought that is so clear in its consequences, the doctrine of Internal Relations is obscure in itself."[4] Rather than try to explicate Bradley's labyrinthian thought, which would involve presenting his whole philosophic position and take us too far afield from the issue at hand, I will present his position as seen by James, the present purpose being to illuminate James's, not Bradley's, insights. Some remarks will be made, however, as to how far James has grasped and answered Bradley's position, or failed to do so.

DISAGREEMENT CONCERNING CONJUNCTIVE RELATIONS

James recognized that Bradley's claim that the conjunctive relations between things which experience presents to us are rationally impossible, was a direct challenge to his own position of radical empiricism. In contesting Bradley's arguments he hoped to refute all idealistic arguments against the thesis of conjunctive relations. According to radical empiricism conjunctive relations are just as real as their terms in a world best represented as a collection, since some parts of it are related conjunctively and others disjunctively (E.R.E., 52). Even though many parts of the world are not directly related, they are nonetheless joined through series of intermediaries, which are linked to each other. The parts that are not now linked even in this way may always be joined at some time by various paths of conjunctive transitions. Rather than the "through-and-through" type of absolute union favored by monistic systems, the world exhibits a "concatenated" union consisting of varieties of hanging-together (*E.R.E.*, 52). Partial, rather than total, confluxes are experienced in this concatenated world. Examples of confluent experiences are concepts and sensations, not isolated, but taken as they come to us, also successive states of the same ego and feelings of the same body. As James says: "Where the experience is not of conflux, it may be of conterminousness (things with but one thing between); or of contiguousness (nothing between); or of likeness; or of nearness; or of simultaneousness; or of in-ness; or of on-ness; or of for-ness; or of simple with-ness; or even of mere and-ness; which last relation would make of however disjointed a world otherwise, at any rate for that occasion a universe 'of discourse' " (*E.R.E.*, 52–53). All of these various relations, which can be found in experience, are denied any reality by Bradley.

Conjunctive relations can be classified as internal or intimate and external (*E.R.E.*, 53). Internal relations signify that two terms are similar in their very nature, and that no change of place or time will alter what they are. The similarity can be predicated of the terms as long as the terms continue. External relations are adventitious; as for example, those of time and space. A piece of paper does not cease being a piece of paper when it is moved from one room to another, or because it was written on yesterday and not today. The paper has changed, to be sure, anyone looking for it in the wrong location will never find it, but it has not changed as to what makes it a piece of paper, but only in its accidental or external relations. Different objects may occupy the same space successively, and the same object may occupy different times, so that neither a particular time nor a particular space are necessarily related to objects. It is this very fact of the externality of so many experienced conjunctions that leads radical empiricism, as a philosophy of experience, to favor pluralism rather than monism in its ontology. Since things in space are seen to change habitat so casually, they can be imagined as so many separate objects unchangeable except in their entirety because isolated. But once things have appeared in space, they numerically add to one another and partake of different spatial relations which characterize them, and so can be said to change them somewhat, but only in that one dimension of their being and not entirely.

Bradley would not agree with the above analysis, but holds instead that all relations are internal.[5] The space relations talked of would be predicated of entirely different objects in that a given predication of position 'A', which holds for term 'X'—the book—in the morning, could no longer be asserted of 'X' in the afternoon, when it was moved to position 'B', because one of the characteristics of 'X' in the morning was its being in position 'A'. Since 'X', which is identified as that term of which it can be asserted that it is in position 'A', can no longer fulfill this description, in that it is now described as that 'X' which is at position 'B', then 'X'-in-position-'A' is not the identical 'X' as 'X'-in-position-'B'. It is insufficient on these grounds to say that the book has merely changed position between the morning and the afternoon; what must be asserted is that the book itself has changed between the morning and the afternoon (*E.R.E.*, 54). Bradley does not deny that anyone using common sense judgment would say that the book looks the same before and after, and has not really changed, except spatially. However, philosophy is not mere transcription of common-sense aphorisms, but is committed to giving a rational explanation for what is usually simply blindly accepted. Although the common-sense approach is very plausible (or else it would not have become the accepted one), it raises as many problems as it solves for the thinking person.

One of the difficulties inherent in the common-sense approach is that it asserts that the addition of a new relation in the result of the given transaction does not make any difference to the terms (*E.R.E.*, 54). But if it does not make any difference to the terms, then how can it be said to qualify them at all? If the terms have not been changed in their inner nature, then how can the new relation be predicated of the terms for no reason? If things can be said to be spatially related in one way at one moment and in another way at another moment, and yet the things are not really altered at all in themselves, having merely undergone an external exchange of relations, then the process and its result, having contributed nothing to the things, seems irrational throughout. If it is asserted that the spatial relations enumerated do contribute something to the terms, then it must also be asserted that they affect the terms internally. If the terms are affected by the relations, then they are really affected in what they are as terms, that is, internally and not merely extrinsically. That in ordinary discourse, and for the most part, it is more convenient to treat some relations as external only is not denied; what is challenged is the validity of such an explanation as a rationally-held proposition.

James answers Bradley's argument that since the addition of a new relation in the result of a given transaction does not make a difference to its terms insofar as they remain the terms, such a relation cannot therefore be said to be true of them, or to qualify them at all. James replies that even if the terms are not affected as to their nature, something is nonetheless affected in that the onlookers of the whole transaction have acquired the new knowledge as to the spatial relations of the terms. Furthermore, the meaning of saying that the terms have been qualified by the changed spatial relations is that they have been changed, not entirely, to be sure, but precisely as to their relative position. Contrary to Bradley's analysis, varying relations can be said to be true 'of' something in a contingent and not only in a necessary or intimate way. The process and its result, rather than contributing nothing to the terms, contribute all there is of the relation. The alleged irrationality of the attribution of extrinsic relations, if it means that the spatial relation is non-deducible from either term singly, can be granted, but without affecting the nature or possibility of extrinsic relations. If by irrational is meant that extrinsic relations contradict the essence of the terms, this contradiction has not been demonstrated to James's satisfaction. The argument comes down to the assertion by Bradley, supported within his own set of presuppositions, that all relations are internal and all change likewise internal or illusory, and the counterassertion by James, likewise plausible within his framework, that relations are both internal and external and that relations can therefore change without forcing their terms to change their nature simultaneously.

Bradley next affirms that the antinomies of space prove its unreality, despite the appearance of many extrinsic spatial relationships (*E. R. E.*, 55). If it would be granted that space were real, then it must be concluded that the world is irrational throughout because extrinsic spatial relations are understood precisely as those which cannot be deduced from the nature of the terms. Since these relations would be opaque to reason and analysis, they would be irrational. Against this assumption Bradley says that there is a reason why one thing and another appear together, and therefore it is foolish to despair of finding an adequate, i.e., internal, basis for change and relations. The reason is to be found in the primordial whole of which the terms and relations are parts and abstractions, and from the perspective of which their intelligibility would be made manifest, since the whole is prior to and contains its parts and their internal connections. Only insofar as the whole is different can the terms attain any difference, since the terms take their reality and meaning only from the whole. If there is a psychological and logical difference between the first and the second state of affairs, as is claimed, then it can only be due to the change of the whole, that is, in an intrinsic and not extrinsic change of relation. Bradley's argument is based on the premise that reality is an unanalysable whole and knowledge an indivisible system.[6] Consequently, any simple description of a single fact is impossible, and even

79

if the existence of facts were granted, they would not be separate and independent; we could not know one fact without knowing another, nor could we get to know them one at a time in sequence. "All facts are necessarily connected: all facts are one fact."[7]

James comments that when terms are altered through changes of relation, whether it is not enough to say that extrinsic changes, of relations, situations, dates, etc., do change the whole, in the sense that when one extrinsic element is changed, the whole of which it is part is thereby changed, although only in regard to that extrinsic change, e.g., it is the man who grows a beard who is said to have changed, and not only his hair, but it is recognized that the degree of hirsuteness does not change the man entirely (*E.R.E.*, 56). The whole problem is one of degree of change, whether it can be partial or whether to qualify as change at all, it must be entire. Bradley's answer is that the change must be "through-and-through" or it is no change at all. If the whole alters, and for Bradley there is no alteration of the terms without an alteration of the whole in which alone they make sense and in which alone they have their reality, then the whole must alter in its entirety. To James, the necessity involved in saying that if the whole, which is primary and determinative of each part, changes, it must change entirely, is one of assertion only, founded not on logic or experience or reasoning, but on an *ipse dixit* of Bradley. James finds that external relations, despite the protestations of Bradley, have not been disproven, but remain both practically workable and perfectly intelligible factors of reality.

Conclusion Concerning Internal and External Relations

James may be right that Bradley's arguments do not invalidate his own position, but this is rather because James's metaphysics is radically different from Bradley's and not because Bradley merely asserts an otherwise unsupported necessity. Within the framework of Bradley's philosophical system the internal relations between particulars reflect the internal relations holding between the universals which constitute them. "To know the nature of a universal 'fully and as it really is' would involve knowing its relations to all the universals which are exemplified in all the particulars which exemplify the first universal."[8] One of the roots of the disagreement over internal and external relations between Bradley and James involves their radically different approaches to universals and particulars. A discussion of the many and subtle arguments necessary as an adequate basis for a choice between a nominalistic and a realistic account of universals, an issue which is still being debated today, was not a problematic in which James wished to be engaged. To do so would mean presenting again his whole philosophy, and he preferred to make a few remarks pertaining directly to relations rather than engage in a lengthy re-argument of his philosophical position, which he felt he had already adequately presented. As has been shown in James's replies to Bradley's objections, from James's philosophical point of view Bradley's arguments against the externality of relations are simply not cogent.

CONJUNCTIVE RELATIONS GROUNDED IN THE FLUX OF IMMEDIATE EXPERIENCE

As with the empiricists, James's most profound area of disagreement with the rationalists, represented pre-eminently by Bradley, concerns the flow of experience. The flux of immediate experience, familiar to James since before the publication of the *Principles*, seemed to him so obvious to mere unbiased observation that he could only attribute the empiricist and rationalist attacks on this most ordinary experience to sheer stubbornness and recalcitrance. In Bradley's case James thought that his ability to perceive separations and powerlessness in comprehending conjunctions was not only stubborn but illogical, as one should admit neither or both (*E.R.E.*, 57). Even an ordinary observer recognizes that isolating certain elements out of the stream of experience for the purpose of analysis does not abrogate the fact that they are separated only for certain specific, temporary purposes. This analysis should not blind us to their combination as originally experienced in the concrete, with their confluence with new sensible experiences. One need only turn back to the stream of sensible presentation to see that the elements analyzed out, the adjectives, nouns, and 'thats' and 'whats' remain experientially confluent in their immediacy. Bradley, however, seems fascinated with the isolated abstracts and does not see their combination as possible. The complex 'AB' is understood as composed of two elements, 'A' and 'B'. The problem is to understand how 'B' may be added to 'A' to form the combination. Starting with 'A', 'B' is either posited, thus losing 'A', or if 'A' is retained, we simply have 'A' besides 'B', with no understanding of how we get to 'A'-plus-'B' conjointly, since the intellect cannot simply unite a diversity. A conjunction in fact merely adds another external element, a 'joiner' which itself has to be accounted for, in that the intellect by nature has no principle of mere togetherness.

81

James thinks that Bradley has the right to impute to the intellect the power of perceiving separations but not unions, but that he should not insist that this emancipated intellect alone has the title to philosophical respectability. Even though Bradley also credits the intellect with a *proprius motus* of transition, he denies that he can find a correlate for these transitions in experience. Neither does Bradley describe what such intellectual transitions would be like if we had them. Instead he defines them negatively, as not being anything like experienced relations, i.e., not temporal, spatial, causal or serial, because experienced relations actually separate terms, to which another principle must be added to unite the terms, and which must further be united, *ad infinitum*. The nearest approach Bradley makes to an intellectual transition is his description of 'A' and 'B' and "united, each from its own nature, in a whole which is the nature of both alike."[9] But this definition is amply demonstrated in the conflux of pure experience whenever anything is given, as when 'space', 'white', and 'sweet', are confluent in a 'lump of sugar'. There is no need to analyze such wholes into separate terms with the necessity of adding a relation as just another entity which itself needs to be related again to each term. Bradley's intellectual transitions seem to be nothing but pale reminiscences of sensible conjunctions which all can experience. The world of particulars are given already united in various definite conjunctions, and there should be no difficulty in understanding such conjunctive unions, since there is no other explanation except the constitution of the fact as given. To look for something more than this is to engage in a witch hunt for an ineffable union in the abstract, a redundant duplicate of what is already possessed in the concrete.

An example of an analysis of the constitution of a fact can be given by drawing out Bradley's abstract presentation of the 'AB' complex in the concrete complex act of a book on the table, which Bradley would analyze into three terms: 'book', 'on', 'table' (*E.R.E.*, 57, n. 14). It can then be asked how it can be explained that these three abstract terms combine in experience just in the way they do, and not in some other way, such as the table being on the book or the 'on' connecting itself with something else altogether. Must it not be said that something in the terms themselves determines the other terms to this particular combination and not just any vague assemblage? Unless the whole fact is prefigured in each part, how can the parts be grasped in just the given combination? The given fact, before existing in time and space, must first exist *de jure*. This is how James understands (in concrete terms) Bradley's analysis of the complex 'AB'. To James this *de jure* existence would consist in nothing more than the addition of a spiritual miniature of the whole fact's constitution in purpose before it is constituted in each part. This to him is the metaphysical fallacy of looking behind the fact for some basis or ground for the fact and finding it in the shape of the very same fact, with the added status of being that fact *in posse*, as possible. This search for a ground of constitution is seen as a superstitious search for invisible ghosts behind visible machinations.

The major areas of disagreement between Bradley and James deserve further comment. The first is James's accusation that Bradley denied the immediate flow of experience, which should be obvious to anyone, and stubbornly held to unrelated monadic elements. The other is James's characterization of Bradley's search for a ground of constitution of facts as a needless metaphysical duplication of a given reality. As to the first divergence of opinion, James and Bradley were both attracted and repelled by each other's positions, sometimes finding large areas of agreement, only to discover yet more divergences. Despite their careful readings of each other's works, their respective outlooks were so different that, except for some broad generalizations, they never seemed to really grasp what the other was saying. An exchange of letters bears out the difficulties of mutual understanding, in this case over the correct transcription of immediate experience.

After reading *A Pluralistic Universe* Bradley was pleased to discover that he and James were more in agreement than he had imagined. In a letter to James, dated May 14, 1909, he chided James for imagining disagreement where there was none, by explicitly affirming what James insisted that he denied—the continuity of the given. "The denial of this is surely not part of the monist's position. . . . Now as for what is given being continuous, *I* have supposed that to be Hegel's view. I have myself now long advocated it, believing it to be his, though I don't say exclusively his. Last winter I read two of Bergson's books. *Données immédiates* and *Évolution créatrice*; and though I found much to admire, I myself was rather *bored* by his insistence on certain points. '*Connu*' is what I kept saying to myself."[10] However, by January 2, 1910, Bradley was already writing to James that he understood the latter's position less than ever: "I begin to wonder if I am not asked by you to start with assuming as true a sort of commonsense realism, and to swallow without demur all the difficulties which belong to it. Of course I cannot do this."[11]

Subsequent to this, in October, 1909, Bradley had summed up his philosophical positions in the article, "Coherence and Contradiction," printed in *Mind* (volume XVIII). James then recognized his own and

Bergson's similarities with Bradley, in that they all "found the real unity of things in that aspect of wholeness which they present to feeling, and . . . laid bare the inadequacies of conceptual knowledge."[12] James likewise still recognized that they parted company in their allegiance to empiricism or rationalism. Even after James had communicated his admiration for Bradley's position to him, Bradley still had to profess (on January 4, 1910) that on James's part "there must have been some misapprehension as to what my point of view is, though here again I don't feel at all clear."[13]

As it turns out, James was also not completely clear on Bradley's point of view. As Bradley countered, he did hold to the continuity of the given. The 'ultimate fact' for Bradley, as for James, is Feeling or Immediate Experience, "a fused-like condition in which all the differences and divisions that occupy our attention in ordinary discursive thinking remain still undiscriminated."[14] "In the beginning there is nothing beyond what is presented, what is and is felt, or rather is felt simply."[15] Although James and Bradley are on common ground in assenting to the priority and importance of pure experience, or Immediate Experience, and to its neutrality as regards discriminations and dualistic distinctions, they differ radically as to the place of relations in this immediately given experience. Bradley holds, convincingly I think, that if there are no subject-object distinctions, nor distinctions of any kind, there could be no awareness of things and their relations either. The world of immediate experience is divided into things and relations, subjects and objects, thoughts and things, only after cerebral cogitations on sensations. Bradley specifically criticizes James for not being critical enough in the *Essays in Radical Empiricism* to see that the neutrality of pure experience precludes all distinct relations.[16] The emphasis is on distinct, i.e., fully constituted and explicated relations.

Even though it seems as if Bradley and James start with an identical premise, and therefore James should have seen Bradley's objections to relations in immediate experience as cogent, their respective starting points are as dissimilar as similar. Bradley's picture of Immediate Experience is rigorously presentational, based on the traditional psychological theory of an idea, sensation or image, being presented to the mind which passively accepts it, while James's pure experience resulted from a dynamic view of mental activity in which attention overshadows passivity.[17] As a result, where James sees relations as active in pure experience, which is in continual transition and not a mere image, Bradley sees only the logical contradiction of distinct relations among objects before objects are even given as such.

But even in relationless Immediate Experience, Bradley admits an implicit "tendency to develop relational characteristics" which is brought out by the contrast between permanent groups of sensations and various variable groups.[18] These incipient relations and terms only become actualized after the self has distinguished itself from its environment and started organizing and dividing its experiences.

For James these "implicit tendencies" are actual relations dynamically operating in pure experience. There is no necessary contradiction in terms being related before the intellectual addition of subjects and objects if subjects and objects themselves are relational events. Furthermore, pure experience is pre-conceptual and the mere tendencies, which are not yet anything for Bradley and therefore irrational if claimed to exist, are yet tendencies for James, vague and unarticulated, to be sure, and therefore not predestined to any necessary outcome, but active nonetheless as real possibilities for later attention and discrimination. The quasi-chaos of immediate relations is still real even though not yet worked out in subsequent conceptual and practical explicitness. It is just this acceptance of pure experience on its own terms which distinguishes James's position from Bradley's. Both agree that intellectual abstractions intervene to categorize and realize relations and objects, but James also recognizes that immediate experience, though vague and indistinct in its pre-conceptual state of inarticulateness, is not synonymous with nothing, but includes real tendencies, which we, in a subsequent categorizing mood, would call relations.

A JUSTIFICATION FOR THE CONSTITUTION OF FACTS

The second area of disagreement involves James's often repeated criticism of rationalists or idealists: that they substitute concepts for perceptual immediacy and then refuse to recognize anything in perception which is not conceptually rigorous, as though denying that a man was ever a baby because nothing in the definition of man as a rational animal explicitly includes a howling infant. James never really denied the value of rational thinking, though he often excoriated its abuses, but he saw abstract thinking as a tool for reentering experience and making more sense out of it, not as an artificial exercise which would refashion the world in its own image. James specifically accuses Bradley of inventing intellectual unifiers to do the job which experienced conjunctive relations are already doing; since the world of particulars is given conjunctively united, it needs no other explanation than the constitution of the fact as given. This appeal to facts as dispensing with the need for theory is a familiar dictum of the empiricist tradition. This trust in facts was never without its opponents outside of the tradition and has recently been under attack from within the walls, as well.

To take Bradley's own defense of his position first—it is meant to answer the objection that the evidence, fact, or experience, go against his philosophical theory. His answer is simply that the identification of such empirical data as facts is itself an abstraction and creature of theory.[19] We cannot justify theory by a simple appeal to the facts, even though not everything is theory. There is a legitimate realm of experience, but it cannot be naively appealed to because as soon as we do so, we are reflecting upon it, interpreting it, in short, conceptualizing or theorizing about experience or the fact. Although Bradley denies that a direct appeal to facts can in itself serve as a criterion to prove or disprove a theory about facts, he does hold that there is a looser sense in which theories of experience can be judged by the extent to which they make sense out of that experience. Even though James sometimes emphasizes experience at the expense of theory, his themes of selective interest and perspectivism, to mention only two, give ample evidence of the overriding importance of the activity of the knower or doer in determining any fact, and not vice versa.

The quasi-chaos of pure experience is a central theme which embodies the importance of the interpreter in determining what shall come to be called experience. The experience itself presents many possibilities; only those shall be called facts which are brought about through a positive intervention. Furthermore, theories are certainly proved or disproved for James according to whether they make more or less sense out of experience. Despite these underlying agreements, James and Bradley still differ radically as to which interpretation makes more sense out of experience. Bradley claims that "the merely given facts are, in other words, the imaginary creatures of false theory" and denies any validity or reality to the experienced world except insofar as it foreshadows a truer, absolute realm.[20] James, on the contrary, praises pluralism for exorcising the absolute, which is "the great de-realizer of the only life we are at home in, and thus redeems the nature of reality from essential foreignness" (*P.U.*, 28). Like Nietzsche, James has no patience for those who would deny the only life and experience we have in favor of some imaginary realm. Unlike those empiricists who take the world of experience at face value, though, James is well aware of the interpretive nature of all our communicated experience.

The attack on implacable objective facts has recently been renewed.

86

Against those who would hold to a direct refutation or confirmation of theory by unquestionable facts, Feyerabend, Hanson, Kuhn, and Toulmin have proposed so-called revolutionary new views concerning science. A quote from an article appropriately titled, "The Theory-Ladenness of Observation," will give an idea of their positions:[21]

> Feyerabend claims that what is perceived depends upon what is believed; and he maintains that among really efficient alternative theories (for the purpose of mutual criticism) "each theory will possess its own experience, and there will be no overlap between these experiences."[22] According to Feyerabend "scientific theories are ways of looking at the world; and their adoption affects our general beliefs and expectations, and thereby also our experiences. . . ."[23] Toulmin, Hanson, and Kuhn concur with this view. Toulmin claims that men who accept different "ideals" and "paradigms" will see different phenomena. He thinks theories not only give significance to facts, but also determine what facts are for us at all. Like Feyerabend, Toulmin asserts that "we see the world through" our fundamental concepts of science (e.g., inertial motion) "to such an extent that we forget what it would be like without them."[24]

Even though James's tirade against theory and the need to justify the given constitution of facts and Bradley's insight into the dependence of facts on theory would seem to place Bradley firmly on the side of the new philosophers of science and James on the side of the traditional view of science, their over-all philosophical commitments justify the opposite conclusion. For Bradley theory not only constitutes facts, it overwhelms them; so that finally only absolute theory is left and all facts are dismissed as chimeras, while for James theory is for the sake of facts or experience and gets all of its sustenance and importance from its ability to re-enter and make sense of experience and turn it to useful or desirable ends. Facts are not so much theory-laden as context-dependent, i.e., our understanding and manipulation of facts is not due to an explicit theory as much as it is to the ordinary way of looking at things, which we have absorbed from our environment, on the one hand, and to the creative vision which we bring to it, on the other.

James's frequent outbursts against theory are directed against the barren theories of idealists who glorify an absolute or logical realm at the expense of the contradictory, messy world we actually have, and should be seen in the light of his conviction that all our experience is inextricably mixed with conceptualization and that all conceptualization should be for the sake of the enhancement of experience. Furthermore, although James says he does not see the need for a justification for the constitution of facts and relations, his actual practice belies the overt statements, since from his major psychological work, *The Principles of Psychology*, to his major philosophical work, *Essays in Radical Empiricism*, his overriding concern has been to make sense out of, i.e., 'justify' by fitting into a coherent framework, his insights into the flux of experience, the givenness of relations, and the dynamism of objects.

CHAPTER SIX

THE MALLEABILITY OF EXPERIENCE: CREATIVITY AND THE DETERMINATION OF RELATIONS

INTRODUCTION

IN A CHAPTER on James's *Pluralistic Universe* R. B. Perry refers to the picture of concrete existence and the picture of a selected world as two contrasting themes in James's work.

> This motive of selection is one of the aboriginal motives in James's thought. It dominated his conception of mind, his interpretation of concepts, and his pragmatic theory of discursive knowledge. Its subordination in this last of James's inspired works provides conclusive evidence both that metaphysics was his central philosophical interest, and that empiricism was his central philosophical conviction—a new empiricism in which philosophy shall depict or suggest reality in terms as close as possible to the sensible flux of unreconstructed experience.[1]

Although I agree as to the centrality of metaphysics and of radical empiricism for James, I do not think that depicting reality in terms of the flux of unreconstructed experience excludes or even subordinates the world of selectivity. On the contrary, the flux of experience is completed by, and ultimately only explainable by reference to, selectivity. James's emphasis in *A Pluralistic Universe* on the flux of experience does not abrogate his earlier and often repeated concern with selectivity, nor is this preoccupation missing even in this book, as will be shown. Perry implicitly refers to the problem which was raised in the introduction to this study, namely, that James inconsistently opts in different places and at different times, both for the reality of the intrinsic givenness of relations and for the reality of the extrinsic imposition of relations. The central problem we have been dealing with reasserts itself here, this time with the emphasis on selectivity, interpretation, or creative activity in relation to the reality of experienced relations or the problem of the malleability of experience in regard to our purposes versus relations as a matter of direct particular experience. The solution already indicated, that relations are really given in experience and yet human intervention is needed to bring them to fulfillment, will be elaborated.

Perry's choice of the phrase, "unreconstructed experience," is significant in that it pinpoints the crux of the problem, the relationship of pure to 'impure' or ordinary experience. As has been discussed, pure experience is neutral as to all dualistic distinctions including that of assigning activity and passivity; in pure experience something is going on, continuous transition is evident, but nothing definite as to content can be elaborated, except as this original experience enters into the articulated and manipulated world of ordinary experience. James favors the sensible flux of unreconstructed experience in his depictions of reality in order to emphasize the secondary nature of all our constructions. He advocates the replacement of free floating theories with conceptual elaborations for the sake of making sense of our experience instead of displacing it, and the replacement of conceptual models of stable essences with dynamic, processive models of action. If unreconstructed experience consists in mere tendencies, then action and even interaction are called for to bring some of these tendencies to fulfillment. Whereas fidelity to the sources of experience would preclude imposition of arbitrary and destructive forms ("Woe to him whose beliefs play fast and loose with the order which realities follow in his experience: they will lead him nowhere or else make false connexions"[2]), the indeterminateness of that same experience would require construction in order to make the experience human, that is, to appropriate and make sense of it. Unreconstructed experience is a hypothetical methodological and metaphysical postulate; constructed experience is the actual lived situation. It is in its spontaneity and continuity that constructed or contextual experience approaches pure experience.

REVIEW OF THEMES OF CHAOS AND SELECTIVITY

The theme of selectivity has already come up in the earlier chapters and will be briefly reviewed to provide a starting point for further development. Personal experience is identified with attention in the *Principles of Psychology*: "My experience is what I agree to attend to. Only those items which I *notice* shape my mind—without selective interest, experience is an utter chaos" (*Principles*, I, 402). Given the chaos of sensation which James, with some reservations, advocated in the *Principles of Psychology*, it follows that the mind must exercise attention and selectivity if it is not to stay in a permanent state of confusion. Since we ignore most of what comes before us, things or objects do not force their being on us, but sensible qualities are grouped and substantialized according to our own projection. The mind selects those sensations which will be considered essential to a thing for its own practical or esthetic reasons and not from external compulsion. No criteria are given for this selectivity beyond the assertion that humanity as a whole largely agrees on what it shall notice and name and what it shall ignore, e.g., the commonly held division of the world into the 'me' and the 'not-me.'

The ethical interest also plays a strong role since we choose what we will become and what we will to become we choose. In explicating the genesis of scientific thinking James emphasizes the confusion of the totality of impressions which we remodel according to the subjective criteria of order, coherence and foresight. The real world as the sum total of all that is going on in the world is literally unthinkable, so it is broken down into manageable groups according to the various disciplines. We impose our order on the world by isolating some relations as essential and law-like and ignoring the ones that do not fit into our scheme. Although James did not offer the suggestion at this point, the reason proposed as to why subjective interests can be said to identify real relations is that nature offers an overabundance of relations, only some of which will be realized. The knower influences the relations which are 'discovered' or brought about.

The problem gradually emerged in the explication of the *Principles of Psychology* that James espoused both an original chaos and an original array of space-time conjunctions. If chaos is fundamental, then selective interest is arbitrary and *a priori* and relations are not experiential. On the other hand, if a given order is fundamental, then the knower is primarily passive and real relations would be given in experience, but creativity would be only imitative, and novelty, ignorance, and conflicting opinions difficult to explain. A possible solution was proposed by emphasizing the complementarity of knowledge of acquaintance, which is immediate awareness of a multiplicity of relations and objects in an unarticulated chaos, and knowledge-about, which conceptualizes some of the vague relations and so brings them into conscious, communicable reality. It was further proposed that a direct apprehension of an empirical space-time order be dropped in favor of multiple space-times depending on the selective interest involved, whether practical, model, theory, or frame of reference. Also a quasi-chaos or vaguely apprehended fringe should be substituted for an absolute chaos, and a distinct perception of relations and objects at first glance be replaced by an immediate awareness of tendency, resistance, and uncoordinated sensations to be followed by a distinct conceptual plus perceptual knowledge-about. These proposals look ahead to James's later writings, and this chapter will explore whether they were developed in this way. Two questions were also raised at the end of chapter one which will have to be taken up: are the categories imposed by selective interest morphological and therefore necessary or are they purposive but arbitrary vis-à-vis given relations, and is selective interest unique to each person or does it follow certain patterns, such as ethical self-creation or body as center of interest?

With chapter two and a consideration of *Essays in Radical Empiricism*, it was seen that a shift had taken place in the central metaphor; James now speaks in terms of experience rather than of the stream of consciousness. With the shift, his theory of knowledge becomes incorporated into a metaphysical outlook. That the world is chaotic now takes on the meaning that the world resists all attempts at unification, whether by a single principle or a unified system. The chaos is not total, then, but partial in that it can never be more than partially unified from any one perspective. The original or pure experience, which antedates both conception and perception, is a process in which thought and thing, subject and object, have not yet been discriminated, a continuous interaction of relations and relata not yet conceptualized or substantialized. Percepts are specific selections out of the undifferentiated chaos. Although no single system can unify all of experience, within any given context or point of view or selected experience, many relations and groupings of things emerge as given or characteristic of that situation. The particular perspective discloses or allows for certain relations in preference to others.

In chapter three it was noted that the central point of the pure experience theory is that subject and object are names for two groups of experiences which we sort 'after the fact' according to the ways in which they act on their neighbors. The hypothesis of pure experience is meant to point out the neutral character of original experience, which only becomes dichotomized insofar as it enters into various contexts. Subjectivity and objectivity are not attributes of reality as such, but the result of later classification. This classification, in turn, is a result of our interests and purposes; according to different contexts different sets of relations come into play. Every experience, at the moment of its actual occurence, at first simply is, only later is it sorted into this thing or that relation. According to the hypothesis of pure experience, there is no inevitable or necessary split of reality into thought and thing, subject and object, but pure experience is the primordial reality unifying all later experiences. The dichotomies are secondary constructs, the means by which persons have recognized and tried to make sense out of the world. We sort experiences according to the different types of interrelation into which they enter. This selection and grouping of different sets of associates is carried out according to our practical and intellectual purposes.

It can be seen in this brief review that the themes of chaos and selectivity are complementary aspects of James's explanation of the nature of experience which have carried through all his writings. The tools necessary for clearing up the inconsistencies of his earlier formulations in the *Principles of Psychology* are provided in the *Essays in Radical Empiricism*, particularly his hypothesis of pure experience. The absolute chaos of sensations is ordered in the *Principles of Psychology* through selective interest, but complete chaos left no room for experienced relations outside of a *fiat* that space and time and other simples are given to the stream of consciousness. In the *Essays in Radical Empiricism* a quasi-chaos replaces the absolute one, thus leaving room for incipient relations, and a selective interest operating out of a specific context provides a means of specifying relations. Selective interest becomes contextualism in *Essays in Radical Empiricism*, perspectivism in *A Pluralistic Universe*, and translation in *Some Problems of Philosophy*. The criteria for selection mentioned in the *Principles of Psychology* are later elaborated in more detail in *Essays in Radical Empiricism*: the body as dividing the world into the 'me' and the 'not-me' and the efficacy of ethical choice. In chapters two and three the importance of the hypothesis of pure experience is emphasized because it provides the crucial framework wherein chaos and selective interest can be made sense of and the problem of given versus created relations resolved. A further elaboration of the themes of pure experience and selectivity can now be given, as well as the later developments of the topics mentioned.

AMBIGUITY OF EXPERIENCE DEMANDS CONTEXT

The pure experience theory signifies that thoughts and things are originally "absolutely homogeneous . . . and that their opposition is only one of relation and of function" (*E.R.E.*, 69). We sort experiences into groups of 'outer' and 'inner' according to the different type of interrelation into which they enter. That one and the same experience can function differently in different contexts is a consequence of the extremely complex network in which our experiences come (*E.R.E.*, 70). This is another way of referring to the chaos of experience in that contradictories obtain there which are disallowed in logic and in a rationalized world. One woman's virtues are another woman's vices, one country's facts are another's propaganda fictions, and one man's vision of red is green to another. Contrary to popular opinion, experiences are not intuitively given as purely inner facts. Their very ambiguity illustrates the thesis that subjectivity and objectivity are not original constituents of experience but derive from its subsequent classification (*E.R.E.*, 71). The classification is due to our temporary purposes. For certain purposes it is convenient to notice and name things according to one set of relations, for other purposes different sets of relations are more congenial. The different contexts in which we find ourselves greatly influence the way we take our immediate world, so much so, that for the most part, no conscious choice or selection is made in our 'takings' of reality. The context defines for us the patterns of reality which we attend to when we do not countermand that context by imposing one of our own on it.

One of the most pervasive criteria by which we dichotomize experience is its relation to our body. At the same time, the body is itself extremely ambiguous as to its function as a material or spiritual center of experience (*E.R.E.*, 76). Sometimes the body is looked upon as a physical object among others, since it can be counted, its metabolic functions tabulated, and its reactions to certain stimuli accurately computed. At other times the body is considered as peculiarly personal, as a center of decision and action and as an arena for spiritual, i.e., private, operations such as memory, desire, dreaming, and thinking. Bare introspection alone cannot reveal to us the materiality or spirituality of the body; for every school of thought that reduces psychology to a branch of chemical-neurological biology there is another that elevates psychology to a branch of philosophical-theological speculation. Still, some bodily experiences are treated as more properly designated physical while others are treated as spiritual or intellectual. The decision for so dividing the body-experience is not arrived at by any introspection of individual experiences but according to the way the various systems of relations behave towards each other and how they function. The various functions into which the system of relations enters "vary with the context in which we find it opportune to consider them" (*E.R.E.*, 77). Different contexts reveal different relations into which the same experience can be sorted. Relations are both given to us already constituted by the context in which we find them and are manipulated or brought forth by our conscious imposition of a different context from the one in which we find ourselves.

The self which we consider to be our own individualized self is itself a part of the content of the world experienced (*E.R.E.*, 86n). It occupies a privileged place in the experienced world, though, in that the world is experienced with our body at its center,

> centre of vision, centre of action, centre of interest. Where the body is is 'here;' when the body acts is 'now;' what the body touches is 'this;' all other things are 'there' and 'then' and 'that.' These words of emphasized position imply a systematization of things with reference to a focus of action and interest which lies in the body; and the systematization is now so instinctive (was it ever not so?) that no developed or active experience exists for us at all except in that ordered form. (*E.R.E.*, 86n)

The answer to one of the questions posed at the end of chapter one has now been given: selective interest, while personal, is not completely idiosyncratic but follows the pattern of the body as center, not only of interest, but of vision and action. We orient ourselves in relation to the world through our body. The systematization of things according to the focus of the body is not a conscious one, although it may become so, but is instinctual, indeed so much so that we only consider experience to be such when ordered in this form. Everything is ordered in personal experience from the point of view of the body, the origin of co-ordinates. The 'my' which identifies personal activities designates the feeling of perspective-interest which suffuses those activities.

Even the supposed independent objectivity of science can be shown to be related to the human body as origin of co-ordinates. I suspect that the recent revelations of deliberate distortion of scientific data, the invention of experiments and mathematical results to fit a preconceived scheme, are only the first cracks in the dike of the monolithic façade of objectivity behind which all the individual referents to actual scientists are held back but not suppressed as is often supposed.[3] The individual perspective is not only operative in the deviant example, which only shows the personal element as distortive, but just as central in the ordinary operations of science.[4]

The Phenomenal Basis of Activity in Creative Effort

Selective interest as a principle of knowing is a subordinate part of the more comprehensive category of action. We do not simply know by mentally selecting specified objects and relations out of the flux of experience, we interact within experience to bring about those objects and relations. Wherever we find anything 'going on' we can call it an activity situation (*E.R.E.*, 82). Bare activity, the bare fact of event or change, is a unique content of experience. "The sense of activity is thus in the broadest and vaguest way synonymous with the sense of 'life' " (*E.R.E.*, 82). Bare activity is predicable of the world of pure experience; the further analysis of actor and acted upon, cause and effect, does not apply to experience in its immediacy, but can be undertaken when the field of experience is enlarged. The notions of activity and passivity, of cause and agent, arise from the fact that in ordinary experience a part at least of activity comes with definite direction, with resistances overcome or succumbed to, with desire and sense of goal. It will be recalled that ordinary experience is experience as it enters into specific contexts. There bare activity is elaborated into definite aspects as we relate it to our body. Bare tendency is resisted, and effort and will are denominated to explain the phenomenon; the activity itself is termed physical or mental depending on how we interpret our bodily interaction with it and is considered aimless or directed according to whether we can make sense of it within the context we are concerned with. The meaning of activity, in its immediacy, is just these experiences of process, obstruction, striving, strain and release.

Having indicated the phenomenal basis of activity, James goes on to answer the metaphysical questions which arise, such as the objection that the feeling of activity does not tell us what activity is in itself, and whether one bit of experience brings the next bit into being or whether an agent is involved.[5] The metaphysical questions stem from the introduction of causality into activity and the consequent search for the constitution of causality. But if we take an activity situation seriously, we will see that an examination of it, without reference to a transphenomenal principle of causality, will yield the very power that makes facts emerge and exist. To take the example of searching for a word or explanation, the very striving to pull into existence the word or sentence which we are looking for seems to be what causes those words to appear. The pulling out of the words from a merely plausible to a real, articulated existence seems to us to be what made those words be. The problem is one of creation, how does the pulling pull, how do we make things be? Everyone is aware of the activity here described as the phenomenon of creativity, but it may still be objected that this feeling or impression of ours is only an indication, a window as it were, through which we can get a glimpse of the real being of cause or creation.

According to a radically empiricistic philosophy, the claim that there are real causal or creative activities must be substantiated by referring to experiences of creativity. If there is such a thing as causality, then it must be experienced somewhere, just as in the case of the sensations of red or cold, which we claim really exist because we can exhibit them in experience. If they cannot be found there, then their existence is a mere possible, a will-o-the-wisp and not something more real, but less real, than our experienced world. Even if it is claimed that we can be mistaken about causality, just as we can be mistaken about particular sensations, it nonetheless remains true that the nature of what we mean by causality can be nothing else than that which appears even in our erroneous experiences as being a causal action. It is just this feeling of causality which must be explained. Creation in its first intention, causality proper, exhibits itself in the sustaining, persevering, striving, and achievement that we undergo. To look for a more real ontological principle of causality, as the preferred explanation of what causes what we call cause, is to substitute a chimera for the given experience.

The nature of causation, as a category of reality, "is *just what we feel it to be*, just that kind of conjunction which our own activity-series reveals" (*E.R.E.*, 93-94). Instead of uselessly discussing what makes activity act or what effects effectuation, it would be more fruitful to solve the concrete problems concerning the *locus* of causality as it is experienced, and tracing and explaining various causal agents and effects, both proximate and remote. James is a confirmed teleologist because he uses *action* as a norm, and the main interest of causation lies for him in the dramatic outcome of the whole process and in the meaning of the various stages by which the process works itself out, rather than in the elements themselves. The nature of efficacy and causality is important only insofar as it sheds light on the deeper problem of the course and meaning of the world of life. In this way the more strictly scientific and abstract work is guided and directed by a more profound motive of establishing the meaning of life.

It should be noted that by situating the discussion of cause in the human situation James has shifted the focus of problems connected with causality. Heretofore, causality and creativity were usually looked upon as diametrically opposed opposites, since cause was considered as the mechanical and predictable repetition of observed events and creativity with the spontaneous and unexplained emergence of the novel. James has collapsed this distinction by considering cause and creativity as identical terms since in human experience what we have come to call cause and effect arises out of our own feeling of creativity, of bringing forth something sought for that until then did not exist. Although we have come to make a distinction between cause in nature and human creativity, a distinction that is useful and workable, James has anticipated the recent recognition in the philosophy of science of the human basis in experience for the so-called objective facts which we have ourselves projected onto nature.[6]

Selective Interest Elaborated as Perspectivism

At the beginning of *A Pluralistic Universe* James divulges an insight that will be the guiding principle of the book: it is that philosophers always conceive the whole world according to an analogy with one or other of its parts which have particularly captured their attention (*P.U.*, 9). The principle of selectivity is openly acknowledged in this book as one of the primordial constituents of the world of experience. No philosophy can be more than an abridgement, a bird's-eye view of the whole of the perspective of events, and the material for that viewpoint is supplied by those portions of the world of which we have had experience. Although each philosopher tends to claim that his conclusions about the world are the only logical ones, they are nothing more or less than accidents of personal vision, which is not to deny that one man's vision may be much more valuable than another's. Indeed, our most valuable contribution to the world is the vision which we bring to it because we will act and react upon it, enriching or impoverishing the world, according to the view which we have of it.

Despite the multitudinous and contradictory interpretations of the world which philosophers hold as a result of their special point of view, there are some deeper features of their approach which all hold in common. They agree in their insistence on being true to the world as they recognize it, they all alike try to make some sense of it and to delineate the features which exhibit its coherence as a universe. What keeps them apart, according to James, are only "small aesthetic discords," different propensities, such as emphasizing security or finality or disconnectedness or statistical uniformity, or the differences may be due to divergent tastes in language (*P.U.*, 11). James can label the criteria for choosing between one philosophical system and another "aesthetic" because all such systems can be ultimately reduced to different points of view, for which no compelling reason can be given other than personal preference.

It should be understood that no appeal is being made to an absolute arbitrariness in imposing one's point of view on the world.[7] On the contrary, James has always upheld the necessity of remaining true to experience as it presents itself. Instead of forcing a rationalistic interpretation on the world, for instance, he suggests that the flux of sensible experience itself contains a rationality that should be paid attention to (*P.U.*, 38). This is not the black and white rationality of logic, but the rationality which emerges from the coherence of parts in the given flux. James rejects the 'block-universe' of the rationalists with its denial of relations which cannot be accounted for necessarily, in favor of a loosely connected universe. The hypothesis of a loosely connected universe is to be preferred because it makes more sense of the world as we experience it. Each part of the world is in some ways connected and in other ways not; no necessary connection holds throughout all our experiences, neither is total irrationality observed throughout. External relations exist because we are familiar with relations that are not pre-included in the intrinsic nature of a thing, which can continue to exist without them, and yet are also found to exist adventitiously with them. The rationalists cannot explain this phenomenon, e.g., that a book's being *on* a table seems in no way required by the essence of the book, except by declaring it an illusion. Radical empiricism prefers to preserve the rationality of the world as we experience it and to find a way to account for it within its own program.

THE FUNCTION OF CONCEPTS IN A CHANGING WORLD

James ascribes a solely instrumental value to concepts and his discussion of this relation of concepts to percepts sheds light on the interlocking themes of experienced relations and creative selectivity (*P.U.*, 122 n. 1). All the content as well as the givenness of reality, both relations and objects, are contents of immediate perception. Concepts are only useful as providing a means of dealing with the remote, unperceived arrangements, whether temporal, spatial, or logical, of the immediately given perceptions. Two points should be emphasized here. One is that James is stressing the importance of immediate experience and warning of the uselessness of mere imposition of theoretic constructs without first taking account of this perceptual experience. If relations are to be found anywhere, they will be found in the immediate flux of experience. That the flux of immediate experience becomes contradictory when translated into theoretic language is due to the limits of that medium and not to the impossibility of experience. However, a second point also has to be made, one which James does not refer to in the given passage inasmuch as it is a defense of Bergson against his rationalist critics. Therefore James is only concerned with reasserting the priority of perceptual experience to barren theoretic construction. The second point is that although reality is only given to us in the immediate flux of experience, as soon as it is communicated, manipulated, understood, or verbalized, it is already 'remote' or mapped out through conceptualization. Thus, although we pay the penalty of solidifying the flux of experience, the reward of conceptualization is the interpersonal constitution of the shared world.

In the appendix to *A Pluralistic Universe* entitled "On the Notion of Reality as Changing" James develops the thesis that logical relations do not necessarily hold in experience. Whereas the laws of identity, of the excluded middle, of cause and effect, apply literally throughout abstract series, they do not apply, except in a loose way, to concrete objects. These have numerous relations with so many different aspects that any principle pursued will have to change in some respect in order for us to say that we are following the same principle in the same way that we started out. In every real series, not only do the terms and their relations change, but the environment changes as does the observer who is tracing out the series. Likewise, the meaning of the various terms constantly shifts so that new types of causation and kinds of sameness replace or modify the old ones to the extent to which they gain our interest. So many new dimensions constantly open out in experience that old relations and terms are dropped or reinterpreted to make sense of the new situation. Experience does not develop linearly, as does logic, but blossoms in many directions at once and in many times at the same point. Although one may be able to isolate series in which logical relations hold by ignoring all those in which they do not, such artificial cuts are only truncated parts of a vast natural network where no such serial relations hold, and can thus not be said to reflect the nature of the world. Not only do terms change, but in time relations also change so as no longer to obtain in an identical way between the old terms and the new.

According to the hypothesis of such a pluralistic universe, science deceives itself if it pretends to give us literally accurate rather than approximate or statistically generalized pictures of the development of reality (*P.U.*, 154). James sums up the conclusion to *A Pluralistic Universe* by saying that "the incompleteness of the pluralistic universe, thus assumed and held to as the most probable hypothesis, is also represented by the pluralistic philosophy as being self-reparative through us, as getting its disconnections remedied in part by our behavior. . . . Thus do philosophy and reality, theory and action, work in the same circle indefinitely" (*P.U.*, 148–149). In these few words James has linked the givenness of relations with direct intervention and healed the antagonism between theory and practice. If reality as we experience it is constantly changing, revealing all the while more dimensions than can be grasped all at once, then the abundance of relations given in experience could be observable without dictating the realization of any specific set. The realization of some relations rather than others would depend on the activity of the experient within a certain context. With even a slight shift of the activity, whether practical or theoretical, or of the experiencer or of the context, different relations would stand revealed. Real relations are given in experience, then, but are only realized insofar as they are actualized in a context by direct intervention. The pluralistic hypothesis remains a hypothesis and not a description of nature, and should be accepted or rejected insofar as it provides a better explanation of and a better tool for interacting with our experience for the sake of the fullest human life possible, than any alternative explanation.

The antagonism arising from the contrary natures of concepts and percepts, which James has been at pains to emphasize, is transmuted into mutual cooperation in *Some Problems of Philosophy*. This book was "the serious enterprise of James's last days, . . . the composition of the most technical and carefully reasoned of all his books . . . it was written for readers, and not for an audience, differing in this respect from all of his philosophical works except *Essays in Radical Empiricism* and *The Meaning of Truth*, and differing from these in being conceived as a unified treatise rather than as a volume of independent articles."[8] James's last words on the distinction between percepts and concepts will also be examined here at the end of this chapter, since they "embrace the final outcome of his dealings with Bergson and Bradley."[9] In the course of this examination, further details will be added as to the working of selective interest.

Percepts differ from concepts in that "percepts are continuous and concepts are discrete," not in their being, for they are likewise active in the flux of feeling, but as to their meaning (*S.P.P.*, 48). Whereas

101

concepts mean just what they mean, the perceptual flux means nothing, although it is much-at-once, containing innumerable characters and aspects which conception can then pick out and intend. Immediate sensible life is unbroken in its continuity, having no more distinct boundaries than the field of vision, and can be likened to "a big blooming buzzing confusion." "The cuts we make are purely ideal" (S.P.P., 50). Attention carves objects out of the original flux of sensations which are then named and identified by concepts. Thus, for the perceptual order, the conceptual order is continually being substituted. Although James calls this substantializing function of conception a purely ideal imposition, he also says that these conceptual relations build themselves out independently of the perceptual flow, then enable the discerning person to single out subtle elements of the flux. These new formations, whether of qualities, relations, or objects, are limitless, and by the means of these conceptual recognitions we add to the store of nouns, verbs, adjectives, and conjunctions by which we interpret life. Different universes of thought thus arise, each with its unique sets of relations, such as the world of common-sense things, of abstract mathematical entities, of practical tasks, of ethical propositions, and of esthetic creations, to name a few. Although the original concepts were at one time generalized from perceptual instances, they have developed independent relations and aspects, which then return to the particulars of our perception which they cause to be identified and recognized. Concepts and percepts are thus equally necessary for knowing reality in its completeness.

In this explanation the original dilemma with which we began again asserts itself: are *a priori* concepts arbitrarily imposed on the flux of sensible reality or do they reveal what is already present in its immediacy, although not in its distinctness? James calls conceptualization a purely ideal cut, which would seem to mean that it is in no way derived from experience, and says that concepts are imposed on the original flux of sensation, and that such conceptual creations and variations are limitless. Yet, he also says that concepts enable us to discern subtle elements of the flux, which are identified and recognized, not created. A clue to making sense of both assertions can perhaps be gathered from the use of the word 'interpretation' to explain the utility of concepts in verbalizing and 'fixing' tendencies. James's position will be analyzed further before a decision is made as to the resolution of this dilemma.

Although conceptual knowledge has been traditionally lauded as a self-sufficing realm, pragmatism insists that its full value is only realized by combining it with perceptual reality again (S.P.P., 58). The more important part of the significance of concepts is not their internal relations and abstract existence, but the consequences to which they lead, either in some sensible particular directly designated or in some particular difference in the course of human experience which it can effect. The priority of selective interest to the mere givenness of sensations is forcefully emphasized by comparing a human life without concepts to a passive sea anemone which receives whatever nourishment the waves may bring, just as a life without conceptions would merely feel each successive moment of experience (*S.P.P.*, 64). The substitution of concepts and their connections for the immediate perceptual flow enables us to widen our mental panorama enormously. Instead of merely mirroring what is given in sensation, concepts enable us to "go in quest of the absent, meet the remote, actively turn this way or that, bend our experience, and make it tell us whither it is bound. We change its order, run it backwards, bring far bits together and separate near bits, jump about over its surface instead of plowing through its continuity, string its items on as many ideal diagrams as our mind can frame" (*S.P.P.*, 64). By the means of concepts we handle the perceptual flux and anticipate its movements. "We *harness* perceptual reality in concepts in order to drive it better to our ends" (*S.P.P.*, 65). The *a priori* imposition of subjective intentions on the malleable flux of sensations could hardly be more baldly expressed. The sheer creativity involved in human cognition as well as in human action seems to leave no room in the explanation of the world for the observance of any experienced relations or objects, nor for any world as opposed to man in any meaningful sense of the word. Selective intervention seems to have swallowed up the matrix of perceptual flux with which it works.

James, however, insists that this manipulation of the sensible flux is for the sake of understanding our percepts better, and not for its own sake. It is the given percepts that we are enabled to know by means of concepts when we plot out the whole system of relations, spatial, temporal, and logical, of our fact (*S.P.P.*, 65). It should be noted that, strictly speaking, distinct relations only exist after an ideal co-ordinated relation network is joined to inchoate tendencies. Before this conjunction we have either a merely ideal system or bare perceptual tendency, both real in their own way and exerting pressure of their kind, to be sure, but incomplete, nonetheless. We translate the perceptual flux into conceptual systems by harmoniously connecting conceptual relations with perceptual experience. Having abstracted or constructed various concepts, we realize new relations between them, which are rational and unchangeable, and then return to the flux

103

of experience armed with these new relations. We interpret or harmoniously connect the mass of perceptual fact with the conceptual series by assimilating the concrete terms of the one to the abstract terms of the other, "and then in assuming that the relations intuitively found among the latter are what connect the former too" (*S. P. P.*, 70). This "theoretic conquest over the order in which nature originally comes" is accomplished by translating the 'thises' of the perceptual flow into the 'whats' of the ideal manifold (*S. P. P.*, 71).

This theoretic conquest is called an interpretation or translation because these words are well suited to emphasizing both the creative and recognition aspects of the situation. Two terms are needed in a translation and in an interpretation, one term that is given in one language or situation and another term from a different language or situation into which the first is being assimilated. Concepts need percepts in order to be effective, just as percepts need concepts in order to extend their scope. Furthermore, interpretations are never adequate or complete. We only assume that the ideal relations hold in perceptual experience; they may not or others may serve better. Insofar and as long as the relations hold, we make use of them; when they no longer do so, we substitute others in their place. Unless a particular conceptual scheme is brought to the perceptual flow, some relations and objects will never be made manifest; in this way the schema is truly creative: it causes something to be which would otherwise never appear. On the other hand, not every conceptual series can tie in with the immediate flux; some are woefully inadequate for handling our experience, which thus exercises a veto over theoretical constructs.

To sum up, in translating the perceptual flux of experience into concepts we gain three advantages (*S. P. P.*, 73–74). The first is that by supplying an immense map of relations, we are enabled to organize the elements of things for practical purposes, both now and for the future. We are enabled by their means, secondly, to revalue our perceptual life and to act according to a new emphasis, and, thirdly, conceptual schemes acquire an independent existence of their own, which can be a pleasing esthetic object. By the means of concepts we can enlarge the field of experience from the here and now to include the future and the past as well as the distant. In themselves, thoughts and concepts are but abstract signs and symbols of things that are given to us as concrete bits of sensible experience. Only by the means of both percepts and concepts can a truly human life emerge and develop.

Because conceptualization has for so long been held up as the ideal province of philosophy, with an eternal worth that denigrates the lowly shadows of perceptual experience, James does not think it enough to show that concepts gain their ultimate value from their relation to percepts, but feels he must point out the shortcomings of a purely conceptual approach and the danger of replacing perceptual experience with conceptual. The central point to keep in mind is that the intelligible order should not supersede the senses but should interpret them (*S.P.P.*, 75). Although we extend our view through the use of concepts and can revalue life by their means, a naive emphasis on concepts can lead us to mistake the symbol for the reality and to falsify our experience by breaking up its flux into the discrete conceptual elements which are cut out from it. Instead of making life more rational, an over-reliance on conceptualization can end by making experience unintelligible. Concepts give us only class names, essences and universals, while the perceptual flux wherein we experience reality is the source of existential particulars (*S.P.P.*, 78–79). At the risk of falsifying reality and losing existential particulars, we must not eliminate the perceptual flux even in the midst of translation. Thus, perception should never be superseded because conception is a secondary process and inadequate to the fullness of reality and falsifies, as well as illuminates, the flux of experience.

Conceptual treatment of perceptual reality makes it seem paradoxical and incomprehensible because we substitute the static relations of concepts for the dynamic relations which hold in the perceptual flux and because the conceptual scheme consists of discontinuous terms which only partly cover the perceptual flux and thus falsify the continuity by naming only parts (*S.P.P.*, 80–81). Among the difficulties in philosophy that have arisen from substituting a fixed relational scheme for the flowing life of perception, those which are pertinent to the given project are that motion and change become impossible, the sense of direction in process becomes unintelligible, and relations cannot be held to be real in the form we experience them (*S.P.P.*, 85–89). Motion and change are impossible because concepts translate a continuum into its discrete elements, which must then be artificially brought into contact again. Our immediate life is full of the sense of direction, but it cannot be known intellectually until the process has been completed, and thus we can only 'know' what has already happened, even though while it is happening we can perceptually discern many directions in which experience is carrying us. Relations which are continuous with one another cannot be comprehended because conceptualization makes distinct concepts of them, thus losing the processive reality of their relations.

These falsifications of experience can be avoided only by making full use of both percepts and concepts and tempering the one by the other.

105

Neither concepts nor percepts can be prescriptive of reality, but the danger for philosophy lies in overrating conceptualization and mistaking ideal schemes for the reality itself. All philosophical schemes, even the most elaborate, like all our takings of reality, whether practical, theoretical, esthetic or ethical, are only interpretations of the full perceptual reality which can never be grasped in its essence, both because perception is too rich and various to be contained in any scheme and because perception has no inalienable essence outside of our interaction with it. "We shall insist that, as reality is created temporally day by day, concepts, although a magnificent sketch-map for showing us our bearings, can never fitly supersede perception" (*S.P.P.*, 100).

CONCLUSION

This explication of selective interest and creativity has completed the argument that James could assert both the reality of the intrinsic givenness of relations and the reality of the extrinsic imposition of relations without contradicting himself. The arguments for the reality of relations both in pure and ordinary experience have already been given in earlier chapters. This picture was incomplete, however, as long as the equally important theme of the role of creativity and interpretation in specifying relations was left undeveloped. The hypothesis of pure experience provides the framework wherein the contradictions involved in choosing between given versus created relations can be resolved so that no choice need be made between the two alternatives, since relations are both given in experience, yet need selective interest to bring them to fulfillment. The role of selective interest has been elaborated through the themes of the context-character of ordinary experience, perspectivism, and interpretation or translation. Each of these themes develops complementary aspects of the meaning and efficacy of selective interest.

CONCLUSION

BOTH the creativity of human intervention and the brute givenness of relations can be upheld after a careful examination of the main themes of James's philosophy. The quasi-chaos of pure experience allows for tendencies and resistances which can be ignored only at our own peril, since the flux of sensation has its own continuity, movement, and sense of direction. These experienced tendencies are the basis for James's claim that relations are really experienced. The incompleteness or inchoateness of these tendencies, however, as well as their very multiplicity and variety, are likewise the basis for the exertion of selective interest and creativity. Which proclivities will be realized depends both on which ones are selected or acted upon and on the ability of the experiencer in identifying real tendencies. The means for transforming the quasi-chaos of incipient relations into an ordered, comprehensible world of identifiable relations is the specification of a context of ordinary experience. This context needs for its realization the givenness of the perceptual flux and the selective interest or perspective of an experiencer who interprets the situation. Thus, the solution forecast already at the beginning of this study has been seen to be workable in detail and capable of sustained exposition: relations are really given in experience and yet need interpretive interaction to bring them to fulfillment.

As has been pointed out, continuous transition is attributable to pure experience, but recognizable relations are only possible insofar as this original experience enters into the articulated world of ordinary experience. Already in the *Principles of Psychology*, selective interest is needed in the exposition of the stream of consciousness to group confused sensations into objects and relations. Since the neutrality of pure experience as proposed in the *Essays in Radical Empiricism* is a hypothesis that original experience is a process in which dichotomies have not yet arisen, subjects, objects, and relations can only be accounted for by the introduction of a context wherein the inchoate tendencies can be classified according to our interests and purposes. A pervasive criterion for classifying phenomena is the relation of experience to our body, which, as an ambiguous center of vision and action, can order time, space, and activity into subjective or objective, mental or physical, according to the way we interpret our own body's activities in the given context.

Activity also unites the two themes of a given experience and selective interest in that the bare fact of event or change is a unique content of experience, pregnant with tendency and a sense of direction, which is in turn resisted by effort and will and becomes a personal, causal, or creative action to bring about a definite situation. Action is thus both given in the flux of experience and imposed as specified projects onto experience. This action or continuous change ensures the pluralistic character of the universe of our experience, which is seen to be loosely connected by part to part, and neither joined by necessary and invariable relations nor disjoined in complete unrelatedness. The multiplicity of relational tendencies in an ever changing reality can be asserted as observable and at the same time subject to development into specific relations through the interaction of an experiencer who brings with him a personal angle of vision or perspective. Changes in the activity of the experiencer or of the context out of which he operates would allow for the revelation of different relations, while purposive choice for stability would allow for the repetition of similar or identical relations.

By means of attention objects are carved out of the original flux of sensation which are then identified and named by concepts. Concepts allow us to plot out whole systems of spatial, temporal, logical, esthetic, and other relations by means of which we harness perceptual reality to make it follow our purposes. This is not a violent imposition of theoretic entities and relations onto an unresisting perceptual experience, but is more like a process of translation wherein we harmoniously connect conceptual terms with perceptual ones. No translation or interpretation will ever be adequate to or exhaustive of the full revelation of experience, which is enlarged and appropriated through concepts but which itself exercises a veto over theoretical constructs by lending itself to such interpretation or resisting it. Perceptual reality is not inert but dynamic and full of direction. Reality is created temporally day by day in one sense by the interaction of, not imposition of, concepts and percepts, in another sense by the interaction of selective interest and sensible flux, and in still another sense by the interaction of context and pure experience.

The use of the word 'translation' should not be taken to mean merely a transition from a physical to a mental mode of existence. Neither should the selectivity of our interests be reduced to solely conscious manipulation of our experience. The interpretive interaction is part of a larger matrix better designated as context. The relations of various experiences differ from one field to another, for instance, some fields or contexts cohere according to physical interactions and other fields or contexts cohere psychically (*E.R.E.*, 270). Within these broader, non-exclusive fields other more particularized or specialized fields, such as emotive, social, or imaginative can be recognized, the cohesiveness of which can be differentiated from the "dull and monotonous repetition of itself in time which characterizes . . . physical existence" (*E.R.E.*, 270). The field of context is specified by the various relations realized in it and the selective interest, as one of the relations, shares the same ambiguity as the others. Insofar as we pay attention to some aspects of a context rather than others, those aspects will be the focal point of our conscious taking of the situation and our entering wedge in whatever externality is being carved out of the given field. Insofar as the context is already specified by previous interpretations, whether by language, culture, conceptualizations, gestalt patterns, neural stimulative responses, or any other aspect of the context, then the selective interest responds to whatever obtrudes. The interaction is totally reciprocal; sometimes interpretive interaction or selective interest dominates, sometimes certain specified relations in the context, but more often, or more accurately, both interrelate.

If the creativity inherent in the ongoing flux is emphasized, then the selective interest of the agent can be discussed as the originator of the novel takings of experience. Whatever we are interested in, for whatever motive or impulse, guides the search in the experiential field for those relations which will realize our particular vision. If the reality of the situation is emphasized as already constituted and the flux is taken as it is manifested in interpreted contexts, then the role of selective interest can be seen as secondary and the test of the successful grappling with the situation will be whether the interest brought to the situation gets ahold of the relations already delineated, whether this solidifying of the flux invokes the context of personal consciousness, a carefully articulated lab experiment, the perambulations of an inaugural ball, a business transaction, or building a house. The rules for verification of the interaction, if any are sought, will come out of the particular context in question or the determination or success of the result.

The interpretation which leads to the successful closing of a business transaction has to really identify the various facets of the deal, just as the identification of the toxin responsible for a mysterious epidemic has to really match the source of the malady. On the other hand, both the business and the medical contexts are full of relations which can be activated differently depending on what is being sought and the way it is approached; there is more than one way to close a deal and more than one element responsible for an epidemic. Depending on the selective interest involved the business transaction can be halted altogether and the epidemic can disappear without apparent reason or be reinterpreted as several related diseases.

Relations are really given in experience and can be identified within a context. Precisely what is given cannot be specified without a context and, conversely, a context cannot be given except as a taking of the quasi-chaotic flux of relations. To specify the context, whether conceptually only, or actively rather than thoughtfully, or some combination of the two, interpretive interaction must be brought to bear. Interpretive interaction operates to specify a context and identify the relations therein just as much when we pick out and buy a box of cereal and thereby give evidence that a supermarket transaction is the ongoing context as when Albert Einstein consciously formulated the theory of relativity. Both interpretations, that of the grocery shopper and of the physicist, influenced and helped specify the context, the former by taking and paying for a box of cereal and the latter by constructing an elaborate theory, and both were in turn influenced by the context because the shopper can only choose among the cereals offered and has to pay the designated price, once he has decided to close the transaction, and Einstein by the experimental anomalies he was trying to clear up.

On the question of the constitution of objects Edward H. Madden and Chandana Chakrabarti are certainly right to reject, with clear arguments, A. J. Ayer's claim that James was a "strong phenomenalist," but it is not so clear that the concept of "weak phenomenalism" is "wholly foreign to his concept of pure experience" and "dramatically opposed to the whole thrust of radical empiricism."[1] Granted, physical objects are not "theoretical constructions" or "conceptual devices," but they are the *terminus ad quem*, the end product of our interpretation of the flux of experience and, as Quine says, the result of "working a manageable structure" into that flux.[2] The concept of objects as theoretical abstractions invented to explain "a primary system of sense qualia" which are otherwise unrelated is certainly foreign to James's thought. But the inclusion of spatial, temporal, and causal relations in experience does not preclude the need to

110

construct physical objects, not indeed out of independent sense data or even out of qualias but out of a wider context which includes "the state of the conditions of observation as well as other factors."[3]

If Madden and Chakrabarti mean that Ayer too narrowly construes the constitution of objects as the imposition of physical objects as theoretical entities onto independent qualia, then they are surely right. A physical object cannot be reduced to an intellectual abstraction, nor are qualia unrelated. But if they mean literally their assertion that "since two minds have the same public object in common, no question of 'constructing' the object in any sense . . . ever arises," then I would have to disagree with them.[4] The "indivisible fact" of 'paper seen' and 'seeing the paper' in pure experience is not given in pure experience as 'paper seen' and 'seeing the paper' but as unbroken transitions within the flux. It is true that "James' act-object distinction is a retrospective one and not an introspective one," but this retrospective interpretation must be explained as well as why the originally undifferentiated experience has been divided precisely as 'seen' and 'seeing.'[5] There are no such originally constituted objects in pure experience as subject and object and our dichotomization of the flux is a later interpretation, due to our interests. Objects are constituted as objects for our purposes and not because they are simply there for the taking. The "same public object" which two minds have in common is an object for them both because they are experiencing the same field of relations and because they have similar interests, for instance, stability, coherence, and acceptance of the familiar. As James puts it in *Pragmatism*:

> You see how naturally one comes to the humanistic principle: you can't weed out the human contribution. . . . We plunge forward into the field of fresh experience with the beliefs our ancestors and we have made already; these determine what we notice; what we notice determines what we do; what we do again determines what we experience; so from one thing to another, altho the stubborn fact remains that there *is* a sensible flux, what is *true of it* seems from first to last to be largely a matter of our own creation. (*Prag.*, 122)

There is "no gap between the knowing and the known" in pure experience, but this is because the act of knowing, as we understand it, does not take place as a fully constituted act in pure experience, but in ordinary, or interpreted experience. As David L. Miller puts it: "Since cognition presupposes prior experience, every interpretation involves a concrete present, a past, and a future. . . . Awareness of anything, including the self, therefore, involves more than one concrete present, since every interpretation of what is present refers to something beyond."[6] Knowledge is an addition to the flux of pure experience, since pure experience is the unmediated moment. The concrete present is the source of knowledge and provides the inter-connection of multiple relations, but the exact specification of some relations instead of others requires interpretation which includes the past and future in addition to the present.

The interpretation can be consciously overt and issue in theoretical constructs, as when the knowledge relation itself is being explained, but it can also be covert, as when action is taken for the sake of some goal and the action takes place within a context which both structures the act as well as being structured by the act. The funded character of experience refers to the whole of the individual's past dealings with facts including cultural and linguistic interpretations he has taken over. We are directly aware of physical objects because we operate within a context of funded experience in which physical objects have their place, just as real relations do. Their place is not independent of our activity, however, and includes both something given and something taken, and the specific nature of their interrelationship has been gradually explored in this study.

Although James has opted at various times for the complete chaos of pure experience and yet for the objective apprehension of a common space-time order, both of these contradictory assertions are part of a life-long endeavor to explain life while remaining true to immediate experience. Inevitably, some assertions made to explain a given problem would be superseded as James gradually developed and clari-fied his unique philosophical insights, and I think that these two claims should be counted among those which should be left behind in piecing together his radically empiricist vision. Likewise, the con-fusion between pure experience as the immediate flux of sensations and as a neutral phenomenon, neither perceptual nor conceptual, was never cleared up by James himself, even though he has supplied the insights needed to construct a hypothetical solution within the frame-work of his over-all position. Indeed, he never swerved from the affirmation of the fact of the continuous transition of immediate experience, which fact grounds all the postulates and conclusions of radical empiricism.

It was claimed in the introduction that the success of James's philosophical enterprise ultimately stands or falls according to whether his doctrine of radical empiricism can demonstrate that "immediately experienced conjunctive relations are as real as anything else" (*E.R.E.*, 45–46). The development of the hypothesis of a neutral pure experience, which has been described as being continuously in flux, exhibiting tendencies and resistances, but which gives rise to specific things and relations only insofar as it enters into particular, articulated contexts, has indeed provided the basis for asserting the same reality for conjunctive relations as for objects. Relations, like objects, are present in the original flux as concatenations of tendencies, and like them, only become identifiable as certain relations rather than others when some of these tendencies are preferred to others by becoming part of a context.

The point of view which structures any experience allows and provides for a definite range of objects and relations, which are experienced as indubitably given within that perspective. If the point of view is emphasized, then the objects and relations can be said to be created in the interaction, if the perspective is commonly accepted and functions as a context, then the objects and relations can be said to be given. Experience in its immediacy is too rich and various to be grasped in its totality; rather, various perspectives allow us to select out of the flux those relations and objects which will form for us a specific context. The relations and objects which we thus identify and name are really given, but so are many others which we ignore; the difference between the two sets of objects and relations is due to what James variously terms the context, point of view, conceptual matrix, or interpretation that we bring to the otherwise unarticulated situation.

NOTES

INTRODUCTION

1. William James, *Essays in Radical Empiricism*, The Works of William James, ed. Fredson Bowers and Ignas K. Skrupskelis (Cambridge: Harvard University Press, 1976), pp. 45–46. Abbreviated as *E.R.E.*

2. William James, *The Meaning of Truth*, The Works of William James, ed. Fredson Bowers and Ignas K. Skrupskelis (Cambridge: Harvard University Press, 1975), pp. 6–7. Abbreviated as *M.T.*

3. William James, *The Will to Believe and Other Essays in Popular Philosophy* (New York: Dover Publications, 1956), p. vii. Abbreviated as *W.B.*

4. Amelie Rorty, ed., *Pragmatic Philosophy* (New York: Doubleday and Co., 1966), p. 361. A paper outlining some of the main arguments of this study was given at the annual meeting of the Society for the Advancement of American Philosophy in New Orleans, April, 1976, and subsequently published in the *Transactions of the Charles S. Peirce Society*, 12 (Fall, 1976), pp. 330–347.

5. For a brief orientation to the difficulty of characterizing experience, *See The Encyclopedia of Philosophy*, ed. Paul Edwards (New York: Macmillan Publishing Co., 1967), vol. 3, "Experience," P. L. Heath, pp. 156–158, and vol. 4, "William James," William James Earle, especially p. 244 and pp. 247–248.

6. Norwood Russell Hanson, *Observation and Explanation* (New York: Harper Torchbooks, 1971), p. 14.

7. John J. McDermott, *The Writings of William James* (New York: The Modern Library, 1968), p. xxxviii.

8. Ibid., p. xxxix.

9. This is taken up in detail in chapter three of this book.

10. John E. Smith, *Themes in American Philosophy* (New York: Harper and Row, Harper Torchbooks, 1970), p. 28, pp. 37–41.

11. Ibid., p. 40.

12. Ralph Barton Perry, *The Thought and Character of William James*, vol. 2, (Boston: Little, Brown and Co., 1935), p. 601.

13. Ibid., p. 364.

14. In contrast to those who hold that *The Principles of Psychology* was

entirely misdirected philosophically and that James's later work negates his earlier psychological phase, (See W. Donald Oliver, "James' Cerebral Dichotomy" in *The Philosophy of William James*, ed. Walter Corti (Hamburg: Felix Meiner Verlag, 1976), pp. 46–47), I side with H. S. Thayer, who says in the Introduction to *Pragmatism*, The Works of William James, ed. Fredson Bowers and Ignas K. Skrupskelis (Cambridge: Harvard University Press, 1975), that the *Principles of Psychology* is "James's greatest work" and "the nexus of almost all his philosophic thinking. From the *Psychology* one can discern the main lines of the development of James's later thought extending into radical empiricism, into his pragmatism, and his analysis of the nature and working of religious and moral belief," p. xv.

15. This footnote appears in William James, *Essays in Radical Empircsm and A Pluralistic Universe* (Gloucester, Mass.: Peter Smith, 1967), 155, n. 1. For more extensive correlations, *See* the scholarly notes and apparatus in *E. R. E.*, The Works of William James.

16. Perry, *The Thought and Character of William James*, II, p. 668.

17. Ibid., p. 507. Among the "youngsters" who have followed this advice and shown its vitality, *See* Michael Novak, ed., *American Philosophy and the Future* (New York: Charles Scribner's Sons, 1968).

18. Perry, *The Thought and Character of William James*, II, p. 387. Letter of February 22, 1905.

19. Ibid., p. 583. Letter of January, 1908.

20. Ibid., pp. 506–507. Letter of May 18, 1907.

CHAPTER ONE

1. William James, *The Principles of Psychology*, I (New York: Dover Publications, Inc., 1950), p. 224. All further page references in this chapter contained in the body of the text are taken from the *Principles*. The references to the second volume of the *Principles* are preceded by "II."

2. *See* the chapter, "Does Consciousness Exist?" in *E. R. E.*, pp. 3–19.

3 "Feeling" is a catch-all word standing variously for percepts, sensations, intuition, presentations, and the immediate flow of conscious life. *See* William James, *Some Problems of Philosophy* (New York: Longmans, Green, and Co., 1911), pp. 47–48. Abbreviated as *S. P. P.* Feeling designates "generically all states of consciousness considered subjectively, or without respect to their possible function," *M. T.*, p. 13.

4. "Unable to lay their hands on any coarse feelings corresponding to the innumerable relations and forms of connection between the facts of the world, finding no *named* subjective modifications mirroring such relations, they [sensationalists] have for the most part denied that feelings of relations exist, and many of them, like Hume, have gone so far as to deny the reality of most relations *out* of the mind as well as in it." The intellectualists, "unable to give up the reality of relations *extra mentem*, but equally unable to point to any distinct substantive feelings in which they were known," also say that the feelings do not exist (pp. 244–45).

5. This argument might be called an ordinary language argument, except

that the appeal to ordinary language has acquired technical overtones due to its co-option by a particular philosophical group.

6. When James refers to empiricists he usually has in mind Locke and Hume. Rationalists include, among others, Kant, Hegel, Royce, and Bradley.

7. In addition to James's recognition of the limitations of language he also expressed a surprisingly "modern" view of it according to William J. Gavin, "William James on Language," *International Philosophical Quarterly*, 16 (March, 1976), pp. 81–86.

8. William J. Gavin explores the notion of vagueness and alludes to context along lines similar to those elaborated in this study in "William James and the Importance of 'The Vague,' " *Cultural Hermeneutics*, 3 (1976), pp. 245–265.

9. For variations on this theme, cf., Michael Polanyi, *Personal Knowledge* (New York: Harper and Row, 1964), p. x, concerning tacit and explicit knowledge and focal and subsidiary awareness, and W. V. O. Quine, "Two Dogmas of Empiricism," in *Pragmatic Philosophy*, ed. Amelie Rorty, pp. 414–18, for the field metaphor of center and periphery.

10. James seems unaware that Kant's distinction between thing-in-itself and phenomenon was an attempt to handle just this problem, e.g., "Accordingly it is only the form of sensuous intuition by which we can intuit things *a priori*, but by which we can know objects only as they *appear* to us (to our senses), not as they are in themselves; and this assumption is absolutely necessary if synthetical propositions *a priori* be granted as possible or if, in case they actually occur, their possibility is to be comprehended and determined beforehand." Immanuel Kant, *Prolegomena to Any Future Metaphysics*, ed. Lewis White Beck, (New York: The Liberal Arts Press, 1950), p. 30.

11. On the possibility of contradictions in nature or that some judgments about it can be both true and false, see H. S. Thayer, Introduction to *Pragmatism*, op. cit., pp. xxxii-xxxiii. James "understood judgments of truth and reality to admit of relativity. . . . Where differences of need and purpose enter in to affect our otherwise common conceptualization of experience, the conditions of meaning and the functions of ideas and the value thought contributes to action may be determined differently. Thus, to some extent (but not entirely, since we live in a world largely conceived in common) we may severally be led to decide that some ideas are true (pragmatically) for some persons and false for others."

12. How does James reconcile this with earlier assertions of chaos? Perhaps these 'truths' are 'ordinary experience' or unreflected common sense which act as limits to speculation—or as the originary phenomena or immediate experience where we have to begin (or return to) in speculation. At this point this is still problematic.

13. A timely warning against juxtaposing knowledge-about and knowledge of acquaintance as two types of knowledge is urged by David L. Miller who says that there can be no such thing as knowledge by acquaintance because knowledge, strictly speaking, requires concepts, that is to say, a reflection on what is immediately apprehended and therefore cannot take place in the immediacy of the concrete present. "William James and the Specious Present,"

in Corti, *The Philosophy of William James*, pp. 59–61. "Knowledge of acquaintance" may not be knowledge, for the same reason that it doesn't acquaint us with definitely constituted objects and relations, but if it is dropped, another term must be substituted, because it points to an indispensable moment in the process that eventuates in conceptual knowledge.

CHAPTER TWO

1.   Admittedly, this analogy limps because the ants are acting in an orderly way whether or not the particular observer realizes it. The point is that much more is given along with the movement of the ant colony, and the scientist selects only those aspects which suit his interests and ignores the rest. The 'key' to what is going on lies more with his interests as ecologist, exterminator, taxonomist, or whatever, than with the multiplicity of sensorial data.

2.   The *a priori* character of perceptual selection is not handled in this account, nor resolved one way or the other.

3.   The claim that actual forces appear to be at work pushing for ever more unification is not intrinsic to the doctrine of radical empiricism, although James likes to link the two. It is a common belief, shared alike by scientists who strive for a total explication of the laws of nature and religious followers who hope for a total revelation of God's ways with men.

CHAPTER THREE

1.   Recent literature has linked James's approach with phenomenological methodology. For a more detailed analysis and bibliography see John Wild, *The Radical Empiricism of William James* (Garden City, New York: Doubleday and Co., 1969), and James Edie, "William James and Phenomenology," *The Review of Metaphysics*, 23 (March, 1970), pp. 481–526.

2.   *See* McDermott, *The Writings of William James*, xxix; Perry, *The Thought and Character of William James*, II, pp. 364–65; and *E.R.E.*, pp. 3–4.

3.   It is remarkable that the hypothesis of flux and change as the underlying character of reality played much the same role in Nietzsche's philosophy. *See* Friedrich Nietzsche, *The Will to Power*, R. J. Hollingdale and Walter Kaufmann (New York: Vintage Books, 1968), no. 51 and no. 520.

4.   Perry recognized the signal transformation of a psychological into a philosophical thesis: "Radical empiricism consists essentially in converting to the uses of metaphysics that 'stream of consciousness' which was designated originally for psychology." Perry, *The Thought and Character of William James*, II, p. 586.

5.   Ibid., p. 666.

6.   Experiments involving infants, in which they respond to flashing lights, for instance, either by a sucking action or by eye movements, provide no proof of an experiential pure experience, since the context of the experimental setup provides the structure within which they are constrained to respond. The infants give us no knowledge of pure experience, but respond to the given stimulus. Within the experimental context the infants' self knowledge, if there be any, is not communicated, but only certain stereotyped responses.

The same holds true for ordinary interaction with infants in which adults 'signal' their messages to them by gesture and voice.

7. In the following quotation James is talking about "the sensible core of reality," which I take to be pure experience: "When we talk of reality 'independent' of human thinking, then, it seems a thing very hard to find. It reduces to the notion of what is just entering into experience, and yet to be named, or else to some imagined aboriginal presence in experience, before any belief about the presence had arisen, before any human conception had been applied. It is what is absolutely dumb and evanescent, the merely ideal limit of our minds. We may glimpse it, but we never grasp it; what we grasp is always some substitute for it which previous human thinking has peptonized and cooked for our consumption" (*Prag.*, pp. 119–120).

CHAPTER FOUR

1. J. B. Shouse, "David Hume and William James: A Comparison," *Journal of the History of Ideas*, 13 (1952), p. 514.

2. Sing-Nam Ten, "Has James Answered Hume?" *Journal of Philosophy*, 49 (1952), p. 160.

3. Ettie Stettheimer, "The Will to Believe as a Basis for the Defense of Religious Faith," *Archives of Philosophy*, 2 (December, 1907), pp. 1–97.

4. Julius Seelye Bixler, *Religion in the Philosophy of William James* (Boston: Marshall Jones Co., 1926), pp. 82–88.

5. Stettheimer, p. 2.

6. Perry, *The Thought and Character of William James*, I, p. 549.

7. "In his lecture at California, James brought out the idea that his pragmatism was inspired to a considerable extent by the thought of the British philosophers, Locke, Berkeley, Hume, Mill, Bain, and Shadworth Hodgson. But he contrasted this method with German transcendentalism, and particularly with that of Kant." John Dewey, "The Development of American Pragmatism," *Studies in the History of Ideas*, 2 (New York: Columbia University Press, 1925), p. 358n. Quoted in *Prag.*, p. xxv, n.41.

8. David Hume, *A Treatise of Human Nature*, ed. L. A. Selby-Bigge (Oxford: Clarendon Press, 1967). Abbreviated as *Treatise*. Hume, *Hume's Enquiries Concerning the Human Understanding and Concerning The Principles of Morals*, ed. L. A. Selby-Bigge (Oxford: Clarendon Press, 1902). Abbreviated as *Enquiry*.

9. Norman Kemp Smith, *The Philosophy of David Hume* (London: Macmillan and Co., 1949), p. 112.

10. Ibid., p. 137.

11. Antony Flew, *Hume's Philosophy of Belief* (New York: The Humanities Press, 1961), p. 112. Flew does not cite the text.

12. Objects can be maintained in belief by "(1) Coerciveness over attention, or the mere power to possess consciousness: then follow—(2) Liveliness, or sensible pungency, especially in the way of exciting pleasure or pain; (3) Stimulating effect upon the will, i.e., capacity to arouse active impulses, the more instinctive the better; (4) Emotional interest, as object of love, dread,

admiration, desire, etc., (5) Congruity with certain favorite forms of contemplation—unity, simplicity, permanence, and the like; (6) Independence of other causes, and its own causal importance." James, *Principles*, II, p. 300.

13. Shouse, p. 81.

14. George S. Brett, "The Psychology of William James in Relation to Philosophy," in *In Commemoration of William James, 1842-1942*, ed. Horace M. Kallen (New York: Columbia University Press, 1942), p. 89.

15. Ibid., p. 83.

16. Shouse, p. 514.

17. For discussion of this, see O. V. Salmon, *The Central Problem of David Hume's Philosophy* (Germany: Max Niemeyer Verlag, 1929), p. 382.

18. This "empiricist" argument is remarkably similar to the "rationalist" argument of Bradley, *See* chapter five, p. 81.

19. H. H. Price, "The Permanent Significance of Hume's Philosophy," in *Human Understanding: Studies in the Philosophy of David Hume*, ed. Alexander Sesonske and Noel Fleming (Belmont, Calif.: Wadsworth Publishing Co., 1965), pp. 30-33.

20. Ibid., p. 30.

21. Ibid., p. 31.

22. McDermott, "Annotated Bibliography," in *The Writings of William James*, p. 843.

23. Ibid.

24. Ibid.

25. James, *A Pluralistic Universe*, the Works of William James, ed. Frederick H. Burkhardt (Cambridge: Harvard University Press, 1977), pp. 110-111. Abbreviated in text as *P.U.*

26. Flew, pp. 138-139.

27. McDermott, *The Writings of William James*, p. xxx.

CHAPTER FIVE

1. James's 'intimate' and 'external' relations are not identical with what is usually meant by intrinsic and extrinsic relations, about which there has been so much controversy. Consequently, some of the disagreement between Bradley and James is due to misunderstanding each other's terminology. For a summary of the controversy, *See* Richard M. Rorty, "Relations, Internal and External," in *The Encyclopedia of Philosophy*, Paul Edwards, ed. in chief, vol. 7 (New York: The Macmillan Co., and The Free Press, 1967), pp. 125-133.

2. About the same time as James, Friedrich Nietzsche also independently pointed out the propensity of grammar to freeze and substantialize the flux of life and of philosophy to blindly copy and dignify grammatical constructions. *See* Friedrich Nietzsche, *The Will to Power*, no. 484, no. 531, no. 552.

3. Richard Wollheim, *F. H. Bradley* (Baltimore, Maryland: Penguin Books, 1969), p. 103.

4. Ibid.

120

5. James's presentation of Bradley's position was taken from F. H. Bradley, *Appearance and Reality*, 2nd ed. (London, 1897), pp. 575 ff.

6. Wollheim, *F. H. Bradley*, p. 45.

7. Ibid., p. 90.

8. Rorty, "Relations, Internal and External," p. 129.

9. Bradley, *Appearance and Reality*, p. 570, as quoted in *E.R.E.*, p. 58.

10. Letter printed in Perry, *The Thought and Character of William James*, II, p. 639.

11. Ibid., p. 641.

12. Ibid., p. 642. Comment by Perry.

13. Ibid., p. 643.

14. Wollheim, p. 127.

15. F. H. Bradley, *Collected Essays* (Oxford, 1935), p. 216.

16. F. H. Bradley, *Essays on Truth and Reality* (Oxford, 1914), p. 158.

17. Wollheim, pp. 129–131.

18. Ibid., p. 136.

19. Wollheim, p. 122.

20. Bradley, *Essays on Truth and Reality*, p. 108.

21. Carl R. Kordig, "The Theory-Ladenness of Observation," *The Review of Metaphysics*, 24 (1971), pp. 448–449. Kordig summarizes the position in order to criticize it—I think unsuccessfully—but the summary is here given for its own sake.

22. P. K. Feyerabend, "Problems of Empiricism," *Beyond the Edge of Certainty*, ed. R. Colodny (Englewood Cliffs: Prentice-Hall, 1965), p. 214; pp. 220–221.

23. Feyerabend, "Explanation, Reduction and Empiricism," *Minnesota Studies in the Philosophy of Science*, ed. H. Feigl and G. Maxwell, vol. III (Minneapolis: University of Minnesota Press, 1962), p. 29.

24. Toulmin, *Foresight and Understanding* (New York: Harper and Row, 1961), p. 57, p. 95, p. 101.

CHAPTER SIX

1. Perry, *The Thought and Character of William James*, II, p. 591.

2. James, *Prag.*, p. 99.

3. For reports of deliberate falsification of data, *See* "An Epitaph for Sir Cyril?" *Newsweek*, 89 (December 20, 1976), p. 76, "Researcher admits he faked journal data," *Science News*, 3 (March 5, 1977), pp. 150-51, and "Eine Ente flog durch die Wissenschaft," *Die Zeit*, 11 (March 11, 1977), p. 20.

4. J. A. Wheeler stirred up a great deal of controversy at the 5th International Congress of Logic, Methodology and Philosophy of Science, London, Canada, August 30, 1975, when he argued that there is no explanation of the origin of the universe possible apart from an anthropocentric one. He said that science cannot escape the inevitable circularity whereby our consciousness establishes the world, but the world is presupposed for the existence

of consciousness. Besides the invited address, "How Did the Universe Come Into Being?" *See* J. A. Wheeler, "The Universe as Made for Man," *American Scientist*, (November, 1974), and "From Relativity to Mutability" in J. Mehra, ed., *The Physicists' Conception of Nature* (Dordrecht: Reidel Pub. Co., 1973).

5. James's mock disclaimer of his phenomenological analysis in deference to metaphysical speculation recalls Kant's warning against the seductions of metaphysics which attempt to go beyond all the limits of experience: "Misled by such proof of the power of reason, the demand for the extension of knowledge recognizes no limits. The light dove, cleaving the air in her free flight, and feeling its resistance, might imagine that its flight would be still easier in empty space. It was thus that Plato left the world of the senses, as setting too narrow limits to the understanding, and ventured out beyond it on the wings of the ideas, in the empty space of the pure understanding. He did not observe that with all his efforts he made no advance—meeting no resistance that might, as it were, serve as a support upon which he could take stand, to which he could apply his powers, and so set his understanding in motion." Immanuel Kant, *Critique of Pure Reason*, trans. Norman Kemp Smith (New York: St. Martin's Press, 1965), p. 47.

6. Thomas S. Kuhn, *The Structure of Scientific Revolutions* (Chicago: The University of Chicago Press, 1970); Norwood Russell Hanson, *Observation and Explanation* (New York: Harper and Row, Harper Torchbooks, 1971) and *Patterns of Discovery* (Cambridge: At the University Press, 1961); Stephen Toulmin, *Foresight and Understanding*; Marx W. Wartofsky, *Conceptual Foundations of Scientific Thought* (New York: The Macmillan Co., 1968).

7. For an explanation of how Friedrich Nietzsche handles the same problem of eliminating arbitrariness in a world of constant change in which there are no facts but only interpretations, see my article, "Why Are Some Interpretations Better Than Others?," *The New Scholasticism*, 49 (1975), pp. 140-61.

8. Perry, *The Thought and Character of William James*, II, p. 661.

9. Ibid., p. 663.

CONCLUSION

1. Edward H. Madden and Chandana Chakrabarti, "James' 'Pure Experience' Versus Ayer's 'Weak Phenomenalism,'" *Transactions of the Charles S. Peirce Society*, 12 (Winter, 1976), p. 4. *See* A. J. Ayer, *The Origins of Pragmatism* (San Francisco: Freeman, Cooper and Co., 1968), pp. 291-93.

2. Madden, pp. 3-4.

3. Ibid., p. 7 and p. 15.

4. Ibid., p. 13.

5. Ibid., p. 13.

6. David L. Miller, "William James and the Specious Present," in *The Philosophy of William James*, ed. Walter Robert Corti (Hamburg: Felix Meiner Verlag, 1976), p. 67 and p. 75.

BIBLIOGRAPHY

I. Principal Works of William James

Collected Essays and Reviews. Edited by R. B. Perry. New York: Longmans, Green and Co., 1920.

Essays in Radical Empiricism. Edited by R. B. Perry. New York: Longmans, Green and Co., 1912.

Human Immortality: Two Supposed Objections to the Doctrine. Boston: Houghton, Mifflin, 1898.

The Meaning of Truth. New York: Longmans, Green and Co., 1909.

Memories and Studies. Edited by Henry James, Jr. New York: Longmans, Green and Co., 1911.

A Pluralistic Universe. New York: Longmans, Green and Co., 1909.

Pragmatism: A New Name for Some Old Ways of Thinking. New York: Longmans, Green and Co., 1907.

The Principles of Psychology. 2 vols. New York: Henry Holt and Co., 1890.

Psychology. Briefer Course. New York: Henry Holt and Co., 1892.

Some Problems of Philosophy. Edited by Henry James, Jr. New York: Longmans, Green and Co., 1911.

Talks to Teachers on Psychology: and to Students on Some of Life's Ideals. New York: Henry Holt and Co., 1899.

The Varieties of Religious Experience. New York: Longmans, Green and Co., 1902.

The Will to Believe and Other Essays in Popular Philosophy. New York: Longmans, Green, 1897.

William James on Psychical Research. Edited by Gardner Murphy and Robert O. Ballou. New York: Viking Press, 1960.

II. Recent Editions of William James. Definitive critical editions identified as "The Works of William James" series.

Collected Essays and Reviews. Edited by Ralph B. Perry. New York: Russell and Russell, 1969.

Essays in Pragmatism. Edited by Alburey Castell. Riverside, New Jersey: Hafner Press, 1974.

Essays in Radical Empiricism. The Works of William James. Edited by Fredson Bowers and Ignas K. Skrupskelis. Cambridge: Harvard University Press, 1976.

Essays in Radical Empiricism and A Pluralistic Universe. Edited by Ralph B. Perry. Intro. by Richard J. Bernstein. New York: E. P. Dutton and Co., Inc., 1971.

Essays on Faith and Morals. New York: New American Library, 1974.

In Commemoration of William James, 1842–1942. New York: A. M. S. Press, Inc., 1942, 1974.

The Meaning of Truth. The Works of William James. Edited by Fredson Bowers and Ignas K. Skrupskelis. Cambridge: Harvard University Press, 1975. Also Intro. by Ralph Ross. Ann Arbor: University of Michigan Press, 1970. Also New York: Greenwood Press, 1968.

Memories and Studies. Grosse Pointe, Michigan: Scholarly Press, 1970. Also New York: Greenwood Press, 1968; Folcroft, Pennsylvania: Folcroft Library Editions, 1973.

The Moral Equivalent of War and Other Essays; and selections from *Some Problems of Philosophy.* Edited and intro. by John K. Roth. New York: Harper and Row, 1971.

The Moral Philosophy of William James. Edited and intro. by John K. Roth. New York: Apollo Editions, 1969. Also New York: Thomas Y. Crowell, 1969.

On Some of Life's Ideals. On a Certain Blindness in Human Beings. What Makes a Life Significant. Folcroft, Pennsylvania: Folcroft Library Editions, 1973.

A Pluralistic Universe. The Works of William James. Edited by Frederick H. Burkhardt. Cambridge: Harvard University Press, 1977. Also Folcroft, Pennsylvania: Folcroft Library Editions, 1973.

Pragmatism. The Works of William James. Edited by Fredson Bowers and Ignas K. Skrupskelis. Cambridge: Harvard University Press, 1975. Also edited by Ralph Barton Perry. New York: New American Library, 1965.

Pragmatism and Four Essays from The Meaning of Truth. New York: Meridan Books, 1955.

The Principles of Psychology. New York: Dover Publications, Inc., 1950. Also Chicago: Encyclopedia Britannica, 1952, 1955.

Psychology: Briefer Course. Riverside, New Jersey: Macmillan Publishing Co., Inc., 1962. Also edited by Gorden Allport. Scranton, Pennsylvania, 1974.

Some Problems of Philosophy. Edited by H. M. Kallen. New York: Greenwood Press, 1968.

The Varieties of Religious Experience. Riverside, New Jersey: Macmillan Publishing Co., 1961. Also New York: New American Library, 1974.

The Will to Believe. New York: Dover Publications, Inc., 1974. Also Folcroft, Pennsylvania: Folcroft Library Editions, 1974.

William James on Psychical Research. Edited by Gardner Murphy and Robert O. Ballou. New York: Viking Press, 1960, 1969.

A William James Reader. Edited and intro. by Gay Wilson Allen. Boston: Houghton Mifflin Co., 1972.

The Writings of William James. Edited by John J. McDermott. New York: The Modern Library, 1968.

III.   LETTERS OF WILLIAM JAMES

Hardwick, Elizabeth, ed. *The Selected Letters of William James.* New York: Farrar, Straus and Cudahy, 1961.

James, Henry, ed. *Letters of William James.* Boston: Atlantic Monthly Press, 1920. New York: Kraus Reprint, 1969.

Kaufman, Marjorie K. "William James's Letters to a Young Pragmatist [H. V. Knox]." *Journal of the History of Ideas,* 24 (1963), pp. 413–421.

Kenna, J. C. "Ten Unpublished Letters from William James, 1842–1910, to Francis Herbert Bradley, 1846–1924." *Mind,* 75 (July, 1966), pp. 309–331.

Le Clair, Robert C., ed. *The Letters of William James and Theodore Flournoy.* Madison: University of Wisconsin Press, 1966.

Nethery, Wallace, ed. "Pragmatist to Publisher, Letters of William James to W. T. Harris." *Personalist,* 49 (Fall, 1968), pp. 489–508.

Perry, Ralph Barton. *The Thought and Character of William James.* 2 vols. Boston: Little, Brown and Co., 1935. Contains some five hundred letters by William James not found in the earlier edition of the *Letters of William James.*

Thiele, J. "William James und Ernst Mach. Briefe aus den Jahren 1884–1905." *Philosophia Naturalis,* 9 (1965), pp. 298-310.

IV.   FOR AN ANNOTATED bibliography of writings on
      William James through 1974, see

Skrupskelis, Ignas K. *William James: A Reference Guide.* Boston: G. K. Hall and Co., 1977.

V.   SELECTED BIBLIOGRAPHY, with emphasis on the years 1965–1976

Allen, Gay Wilson. *William James: A Biography.* New York: the Viking Press, 1967, 1969.

———, ed. and intro. *A William James Reader.* Boston: Houghton Mifflin Co., 1972.

Anderson, Paul Russell and Fisch, M. H. *Philosophy in America from the Puritans to James, with Representative Selections.* New York: Octagon Books, 1969.

Anscombe, G. E. M. "The Subjectivity of Sensation." *Ajatus.* 36 (1974), pp. 3–18.

Ayer, A. J. *The Origins of Pragmatism.* Studies in the Philosophy of Charles Sanders Peirce and William James. San Francisco: Freeman, Cooper and Co., 1968.

Baumgarten, Edward. *Der Pragmatismus: R. W. Emerson, W. James, J. Dewey.* Frankfurt am Main: V. Klostermann, 1938.

Bayley, James E. "A Jamesian Theory of Self." *Transactions of the Charles S. Peirce Society.* 12 (Spring, 1976), pp. 148–165.

Beard, Robert W. "James and the Rationality of Determinism." *Journal of the History of Philosophy,* 5 (April, 1967), pp. 149–156.

————. "James' Notion of Rationality." *Darshana International,* 6 (1967), pp. 6–12.

————. "*The Will to Believe* Revisited." *Ratio,* 8 (1966), pp. 169–179.

Beck, Lewis White. *Six Secular Philosophers: Religious Themes in the Thought of Spinoza, Hume, Kant, Nietzsche, William James, Santayana.* New York: The Free Press, 1966.

Bentley, Arthur F. "The Jamesian Datum." *Inquiry Into Inquiries.* Edited by Sydney Ratner. Boston: The Beacon Press, 1954, pp. 230–267.

Bixler, J. S. " 'Relevance' in the Philosophy of William James." *Religious Humanism,* 9 (Winter, 1975), pp. 38–44.

Bixler, Julius Seelye. *Religion in the Philosophy of William James.* Boston: Marshall Jones Co., 1926.

Blomberg, Jaakko. "James on Belief and Truth." *Ajatus,* 31 (1969), pp. 171–187.

Boutroux, Emile. *William James.* London: Longmans, Green, 1912.

Bradley, Francis Herbert. *Appearance and Reality.* London, 1893; 2nd ed., 1897.

————. *Collected Essays.* Oxford, 1935.

————. *Ethical Studies.* Oxford, 1876; 2nd ed., 1927.

————. *Essays on Truth and Reality.* Oxford, 1914.

————. *Principles of Logic.* Oxford, 1883; 2nd ed., 1922.

Brennan, Bernard P. *The Ethics of William James.* New York: Bookman Assoc., 1961.

————. *William James.* New York: Twayne Pub., 1968. New Haven: College and University Press Services, 1971.

Bridges, Leonard Hal. *American Mysticism: from William James to Zen.* New York: Harper and Row, 1970.

Browning, Douglas, ed. *Philosophers of Process.* New York: Random House, 1965.

Carnap, Rudolf. "Empiricism, Semantics and Ontology." *Pragmatic Philosophy,* Edited by Amelie Rorty, pp. 396–411.

Chakrabarti, Chandana. "James and the Identity Theory." *Behaviorism,* 3 (Fall, 1975), pp. 152–155.

Chamberlain, Gary L. "The Drive for Meaning in William James' Analysis of Religious Experience." *The Journal of Value Inquiry,* 5 (Summer, 1971), pp. 194–206.

Colodny, R., ed. *Beyond the Edge of Certainty.* Englewood Cliffs: Prentice Hall, 1965.

Compton, Charles Herrick. *William James, Philosopher and Man.* New York: Scarecrow Press, 1957.

Corti, Walter Robert, ed. *The Philosophy of William James.* Hamburg: Felix Meiner Verlag, 1976.

Datta, S. *The Problem of Relation in Contemporary Philosophy.* Allahabad: The University Press, n.d. (Original doctoral thesis, 1940).

De Aloysio, Francesco. *Da Dewey a James.* Rome: Bulzoni, 1972.

Dalaney, Cornelius F. "Recent Work on American Philosophy." *New Scholasticism,* 45 (Summer, 1971), pp. 457–477.

Dilworth, D. "The Initial Formations of 'Pure Experience' in Nishida Kitaro and William James." *Monumenta Nipponica,* 24 (1969), pp. 93–111.

Dooley, Patrick K. "The Nature of Belief: The Proper Context for James' *The Will to Believe.*" *Transactions of the Charles S. Peirce Society,* 8 (Summer, 1972), 141–151.

———. *Pragmatism as Humanism: The Philosophy of William James.* Chicago: Nelson-Hall, 1974.

Edie, James M. "The Genesis of a Phenomenological Theory of the Experience of Personal Identity: William James on Consciousness and the Self." *Man and World,* 6 (September, 1973), pp. 322–338.

———. ed. and intro. *An Invitation to Phenomenology: Studies in the Philosophy of Experience.* Chicago: Quadrangle Books, 1965.

———. "John Wild's Interpretation of William James's Theory of the Free Act." *Man and World,* 8 (May, 1975), pp. 136–140.

———. ed. and intro. *New Essays in Phenomenology. Studies in the Philosophy of Experience.* Chicago: Quadrangle Books, 1969.

———. "William James and Phenomenology." *The Review of Metaphysics,* 23 (March, 1970), pp. 481–526.

Eisendrath, Craig R. *The Unifying Moment: The Psychological Philosophy of William James and Alfred North Whitehead.* Cambridge: Harvard University Press, 1971.

Essays Philosophical and Psychological: in Honor of William James, by his colleagues at Columbia University. London: Longman's Green and Co., 1908.

Fairbanks, Matthew. "Wittgenstein and James." *New Scholasticism,* 40 (1966), pp. 331–340.

Feigl, H. and Maxwell, G. *Minnesota Studies in the Philosophy of Science.* Minneapolis: University of Minnesota Press, 1962.

Fernandez, Pelayo Hipolito. *Miguel de Unamuno y William James: un Paralelo Pragmatico.* Salamanca: Cervantes, 1961.

Feyerabend, P. K. "An Attempt at a Realistic Interpretation of Experience." *Proceedings of the Aristotelian Society,* 1957–58.

Fisher, John J. "Santayana on James: A Conflict of Views on Philosophy." *American Philosophical Quarterly,* 2 (1965), pp. 67–73.

Fizer, John. "Ingarden's Pases, Bergson's Duree Reele, and William James' Stream: Metaphoric Variants on Mutually Exclusive Concepts on the Theme of Time." *Dialectics and Humanism,* 2 (Summer, 1975), pp. 33–48.

Flew, Antony. *Hume's Philosophy of Belief.* New York: The Humanities Press, 1961.

Flournoy, Theodore. *The Philosophy of William James.* Freeport, New York:

Books for Libraries Press, 1969. Reprint of 1917 edition.

Gavin, William J. "William James and the Importance of 'The Vague.' " *Cultural Hermeneutics*, 3 (1976), pp. 245–265.

———. "William James on Language." *International Philosophical Quarterly*, 16 (March, 1976), pp. 81–86.

Gini, A. R. "Radical Subjectivism in the Thought of William James." *The New Scholasticism*, 48 (Autumn, 1974), pp. 509–518.

Giuffrida, Robert. "James on Meaning and Significance." *Transactions of the Charles S. Peirce Society*, 11 (Winter, 1975), pp. 18–36.

Gobar, Ash. "History of the Phenomenological Trend in the Philosophy and Psychology of William James (1842–1910)." *American Philosophical Society Yearbook*, (1968), pp. 582–583.

———. "The Phenomenology of William James." *Proceedings of the American Philosophical Society*, 114 (1970), pp. 294–309.

Gould, James A. "R. B. Perry on the Origin of American and European Pragmatism." *Journal of the History of Philosophy*, 8 (October, 1970), pp. 431–450.

Grattan, Clinton Hartley. *The Three Jameses, A Family of Minds: Henry James, Sr., William James, Henry James.* New York: University Press, 1962.

Grene, Marjorie. *The Knower and the Known.* Berkeley: University of California Press, 1974.

Gurwitsch, Aron. *The Field of Consciousness.* Pittsburgh: Duquesne University Press, 1964.

Hanson, Norwood Russell. *Observation and Explanation.* New York: Harper and Row, Harper Torchbooks, 1971.

Hare, Peter H. and Madden, Edward H. "William James, Dickinson Miller and C. Ducasse on the Ethics of Belief." *Transactions of the Charles S. Peirce Society*, 4 (Fall, 1968), pp. 115–129.

Hausman, Alan. "Hume's Theory of Relations." *Nous*, 1 (August, 1967), pp. 255–282.

Helm, Bertrand P. "William James on the Nature of Time." *Tulane Studies in Philosophy*, 24 (1975), pp. 33–47.

Hertz, Richard A. "James and Moore: Two Perspectives on Truth." *Journal of the History of Philosophy*, 9 (April, 1971), pp. 213–221.

Hocks, Richard A. *Henry James and Pragmatic Thought: a Study in the Relationship Between the Philosophy of William James and the Literary Art of Henry James.* Chapel Hill: The University of North Carolina Press, 1974.

Hoffding, Harald. *Moderne Philosophen.* Vorlesungen, gehalten an der Universitaet in Kopenhagen im Herbst 1902. Leipzig: O. R. Reisland, 1905.

Hume, David. *Hume's Enquiries Concerning the Human Understanding and Concerning the Principles of Morals.* Edited by L. A. Selby-Bigge. Oxford: Clarendon Press, 1902.

———. *A Treatise of Human Nature.* Edited by L. A. Selby-Bigge. Oxford: Clarendon Press, 1967.

Johnson, Ellwood. "William James and the Art of Fiction." *The Journal of Aesthetics and Art Criticism*, 30 (Spring, 1972), pp. 285–296.

Kallen, Horace M., ed. *In Commemoration of William James. 1842–1942.* New York: Columbia University Press, 1942.

———. *William James and Henri Bergson: A Study in Contrasting Theories of Life.* Chicago: University of Chicago Press, 1914.

Kant, Immanuel. *Prolegomena to Any Future Metaphysics.* Edited by Lewis White Beck. New York: The Liberal Arts Press, 1950.

———. *Critique of Pure Reason.* Trans. by Norman Kemp Smith. New York: St. Martin's Press, 1965.

Kauber, Peter. "The Development of the New Pragmatic Theory of the *A Priori.*" *Kinesis*, 3 (Fall, 1970), pp. 9–33.

———. "Does James's Ethics of Belief Rest on a Mistake?" *Southern Journal of Philosophy*, 12 (Summer, 1974), pp. 201–214.

———. "The Foundations of James's Ethics of Belief." *Ethics*, 84 (January, 1974), pp. 151–166.

Kauber, Peter and Hare, P. H. "The Right and Duty to Will to Believe." *Canadian Journal of Philosophy*, 4 (December, 1974), pp. 327–343.

Kersten, Fred. "Franz Brentano and William James." *Journal of the History of Philosophy*, 7 (April, 1969), pp. 177–191.

Kordig, Carl R. "The Theory-Ladenness of Observation." *The Review of Metaphysics*, 24 (1971), pp. 448–84.

Kuhn, Thomas S. *The Structure of Scientific Revolutions.* Chicago: The University of Chicago Press, 1970.

Lewis, C. I. "A Pragmatic Conception of the *A Priori.*" *Pragmatic Philosophy*, Edited by Amelie Rorty, pp. 352–61.

Linschoten, Johannes. *On the Way Toward a Phenomenological Psychology: the Psychology of William James.* Edited by Amadeo Giorgi. Pittsburgh: Dusquesne University Press, 1968.

MacLeod, William J. "James' Will to Believe, Revisited." *Personalist*, 48 (April, 1967), pp. 149–166.

Madden, Edward H. "Chauncey Wright and the Concept of the Given." *Transactions of the Charles S. Peirce Society*, 8 (Winter, 1972), pp. 48–52.

Madden, Edward H. and Chakrabarti, Chandana. "James' 'Pure Experience' versus Ayer's 'Weak Phenomenalism.' " *Transactions of the Charles S. Peirce Society*, 12 (Winter, 1976), pp. 3–17.

Marshall, G. D. "Attention and Will." *Philosophical Quarterly*, 20 (January, 1970), pp. 14–25.

Martland, Thomas R., Jr. *The Metaphysics of William James and John Dewey: Process and Structure in Philosophy and Religion.* New York: Philosophical Library, 1964.

Mathur, Dinesh Chandra. *Naturalistic Philosophies of Experience: Studies in James, Dewey and Farber against the Background of Husserl's Phenomenology.* St. Louis: Warren H. Green, 1971.

McDermott, John J., ed. *The Writings of William James.* New York: The

Modern Library, 1968.

Meyers, Gerald E. "William James on Time Perception." *Philosophy of Science*, 38 (September, 1971), pp. 353–360.

Meyers, Robert G. "Ayer on Pragmatism." *Metaphilosophy*, 6 (January, 1975), pp. 44–53.

———. "Meaning and Metaphysics in James." *Philosophy and Phenomenological Research*, 31 (March, 1971), pp. 369–380.

———. "Natural Realism and Illusion in James's Radical Empiricism." *Transactions of the Charles S. Peirce Society*, 5 (Fall, 1969), pp. 211–223.

Moore, Edward C. *American Pragmatism: Peirce, James and Dewey.* New York: Columbia University Press, 1961.

———. *William James.* New York: Washington Square Press, 1965.

Morris, Lloyd. *William James: The Message of a Modern Mind.* New York: Charles Scribner's Sons, 1950.

Mullin, Richard P., Jr. "Does Speculative Philosophy Make a Difference: Jamesian Approach to the Justification of Metaphysics." *Journal of the West Virginia Philosophical Society*, (Spring, 1975), pp. 19–21.

Murphey, Murray G. "Kant's Children, the Cambridge Pragmatists." *Transactions of the Charles S. Peirce Society*, 4 (Winter, 1968), pp. 3–33.

Myers, Gerald E. "William James on Time Perception." *Philosophy of Science*, 38 (September, 1971), pp. 353–360.

Newman, Jay. "The Faith of Pragmatists." *Sophia*, 13 (April, 1974), pp. 1–15.

Nietzsche, Friedrich. *The Will to Power.* Edited by Walter Kaufmann. New York: Vintage Books, 1968.

Novak, Michael, ed. *American Philosophy and the Future. Essays for a New Generation.* New York: Charles Scribner's Sons, 1968.

Pancheri, Lillian U. "James, Lewis and the Pragmatic *A Priori*." *Transactions of the Charles S. Peirce Society*, 7 (Summer, 1971), pp. 135–149.

Perry, Ralph Barton. *In the Spirit of William James.* Bloomington: Indiana University Press, 1958.

———. *Present Philosophical Tendencies.* New York: Greenwood Press, 1968.

———. *The Thought and Character of William James.* 2 vols. Boston: Little, Brown, and Co., 1935.

Phillips, D. C. "James, Dewey, and the Reflex Arc." *Journal of the History of Ideas*, 32 (1971), pp. 555–568.

Polanyi, Michael. *Personal Knowledge.* New York: Harper and Row, 1964.

Quine, W. V. O. "Two Dogmas of Empiricism." *The Philosophical Review*, 60 (1951). Abridged version reprinted in Rorty, ed. *Pragmatic Philosophy.*

Ratner, Sidney, ed. *Inquiry Into Inquiries.* Boston: The Beacon Press, 1954.

Reck, Andrew J. "Dualism in William James's *Principles of Psychology*." *Tulane Studies in Philosophy*, 21 (1972), pp. 23–38.

———. "Epistemology in William James's *Principles of Psychology*." *Tulane Studies in Philosophy*, 22 (1973), pp. 79–115.

———. *Introduction to William James. An Essay and Selected Texts.* Bloomington: Indiana University Press, 1967.

———. The Philosophical Psychology of William James." *Southern Journal of Philosophy*, 9 (Fall, 1971), pp. 293–312.

———. *William James et l'attitude Pragmatiste.* Paris: Seghers, 1967.

Reeve, E. Gavin. "William James on Pure Being and Pure Nothing." *Philosophy*, 45 (January, 1970), pp. 59–60.

Riconda, Guiseppe. "L'empirismo radicale di William James. *Filosofia*, 16 (1965), pp. 291–332.

———. "La filosofia della religione di William James. *Filosofia*, 15 (1964), pp. 241–277.

Riepe, Dale, "A Note on William James and Indian Philosophy." *Philosophy and Phenomenological Research*, 28 (June, 1968), pp. 587–590.

Roberts, James Deotis. *Faith and Reason: A Comparative Study of Pascal, Bergson, and James.* Boston: Christopher Publishing House, 1962.

Roggerone, Giuseppe Agostino. *James e la crisi della conscienza contemporanea.* Milano: Marzorati, 1967.

Rorty, Amelie, ed. *Pragmatic Philosophy.* New York: Doubleday and Co., 1966.

Rorty, Richard M. "Relations, Internal and External." *The Encyclopedia of Philosophy.* 1967. Vol. VII.

Rosenthal, Sandra B. "C. I. Lewis and Radical Empiricism." *Transactions of Charles S. Peirce Society*, 8 (Spring, 1972), pp. 106–14.

———. "Recent Perspectives on American Pragmatism." Part I. *Transactions of the Charles S. Peirce Society*, 10 (Spring, 1974), pp. 76–93. Part II. 10 (Summer, 1974), pp. 166–184.

Ross, Robert R. N. "William James: The Wider Consciousness." *Philosophy Today*, 20 (Summer, 1976), pp. 134–148.

Roth, John K. *Freedom and the Moral Life: the Ethics of William James.* Philadelphia: Westminster Press, 1969.

Roth, Robert J. "Is Peirce's Pragmatism Anti-Jamesian?" *International Philosophical Quarterly*, 5 (1965), pp. 541–563.

———. "The Religious Philosophy of William James." *Thought*, 41 (1966), pp. 249–281.

Royce, Josiah. *William James and Other Essays on the Philosophy of Life.* Reprint of 1911 edition. Freeport, New York: Books for Libraries, 1969.

Salmon, C. V. *The Central Problem of David Hume's Philosophy.* Germany: Max Niemeyer Verlag, 1929.

Scheffler, Israel. *Four Pragmatists: A Critical Introduction to Peirce, James Mead, and Dewey.* New York: Humanities Press, 1974.

Schirmer, D. B. "William James and the New Age." *Science and Society*, 33 (1969), pp. 434–445.

Schmidt, Hermann. *Der Begriff der Erfahrungskontinuitaet bei William James und seine Bedeutung fuer den amerikanischen Pragmatismus.* Heidelberg: C. Winter Verlag, 1959.

Schrag, Calvin O. "Struktur der Erfahrung in der Philosophie von James und Whitehead." *Zeitschrift für philosophische Forschung*, 23 (1969), pp. 479–494.

Seigfried, Charlene Haddock. "The Structure of Experience for William James." *Transactions of the Charles S. Peirce Society*, 12 (Fall, 1976), pp. 330–347.

———. "Why Are Some Interpretations Better Than Others?" *The New Scholasticism*, 49 (Spring, 1975), pp. 140–161.

Sesonske, Alexander and Fleming, Noel. *Human Understanding: Studies in the Philosophy of David Hume*. Belmont, California: Wadsworth Publishing Co., 1965.

Shields, Allan. "On a Certain Blindness in William James and Others." *Journal of Aesthetics and Art Criticism*, 27 (Fall, 1968), pp. 27–34.

Shouse, J. B. "David Hume and William James: A Comparison." *Journal of the History of Ideas*. 13 (1952), pp. 514–527.

Singer, Marcus G. "The Pragmatic Use of Language and the *Will to Believe*." *American Philosophical Quarterly*, 8 (January, 1971), pp. 24–34.

Skousgaard, Stephen. "The Phenomenology in William James' Philosophical Psychology." *The Journal of the British Society of Phenomenology*, 7 (May, 1976), pp. 86–95.

Smith, John E. "The Reflexive Turn, the Linguistic Turn, and the Pragmatic Outcome." *Monist*, 53 (October, 1969), pp. 588–605.

———. *The Spirit of American Philosophy*. Oxford University Press, 1963.

———. *Themes in American Philosophy: Purpose, Experience and Community*. New York: Harper and Row, Harper Torchbooks, 1960.

Smith, Norman Kemp. *The Philosophy of David Hume*. London: Macmillan and Co., 1949.

Spicker, Stuart F. "William James and Phenomenology." *The Journal of the British Society for Phenomenology*, 2 (1971), pp. 69–74. Bruce Wilshire, "A Reply," pp. 75–80. S. F. Spicker, "Brief Rejoinder to Mr. Wilshire," p. 80.

Stettheimer, Ettie. "*The Will to Believe* as a Basis for the Defense of Religious Faith." *Archives of Philosophy*, 2 (December, 1907), pp. 1–97.

Stevens, Richard. *James and Husserl: The Foundations of Meaning*. The Hague: Martinus Nijhoff, 1974.

Strout, C. "William James and the Twice-born Sick Soul." *Daedalus*, 97 (1968), pp. 1062–1082.

Ten, Sing-Nam. "Has James Answered Hume?" *Journal of Philosophy*, 49 (1952), p. 160.

Thayer, H. S. *Meaning and Action: A Critical History of Pragmatism*. Indianapolis: Bobbs-Merrill, 1968.

Tibbits, Paul. "The Philosophy of Science of William James: An Unexplored Dimension of James' Thought." *Personalist*, 52 (Summer, 1971), pp. 535–556.

Toulmin, Stephen. *Foresight and Understanding*. New York: Harper and Row, 1961.

Wartofsky, Marx W. *Conceptual Foundations of Scientific Thought.* New York: The Macmillan Co., 1968.

Weinstein, Michael A. "Life and Politics as Plural: James and Bentley on the Twentieth Century Problem." *Journal of Value Inquiry,* 5 (1970–1971), pp. 282–291.

Wertz, Spencer K. "On Wittgenstein and James." *The New Scholasticism,* 46 (Autumn, 1972), pp. 446–448.

Wickham, Harvey. *The Unrealists: James, Bergson, Santayana, Einstein, Bertrand Russell, John Dewey, Alexander and Whitehead.* Reprint of the 1930 edition. Freeport, New York: Books for Libraries, 1970. Also Port Washington, New York: Kennikat Press, 1971.

Wild, John. *The Radical Empiricism of William James.* Garden City, New York: Doubleday and Co., Inc., 1969.

———. "William James and Existential Authenticity." *Journal of Existentialism,* 5 (1964–1965), pp. 243–256.

Wilshire, Bruce. "Protophenomenology in the Psychology of William James." *Transactions of the Charles S. Peirce Society,* 5 (Winter, 1969), pp. 25–43.

———. "A Reply to Stuart Spicker's 'William James and Phenomenology.' " *The Journal of the British Society for Phenomenology,* 2 (October, 1971), pp. 75–80.

———. *William James and Phenomenology: A Study of the Principles of Psychology.* Bloomington: Indiana University Press, 1968.

Wollheim, Richard. *F. H. Bradley.* Baltimore, Maryland: Penguin Books, 1969.

Zabeeh, Farhang. *Hume: Precursor of Modern Empiricism.* Netherlands: Martinus Nijhoff, 1960.

INDEX

Hegel, 71, 117
Hodgson, Shadworth, 119
Hume, xii, 6, 10, 14, 54-69, 71, 75, 116, 117, 119
Husserl, ix
Identity: of subject and object, 17-18
Interest, *See* Selective interest
Interpretation, 29, 47, 86, 90, 102, 104, 106, 108-113; *See also* Translation
Inquiry Concerning Human Understanding, An (Hume), 55-59, 66-68
Kant, 6, 40, 55, 117, 119, 122
Knowledge-about: definition of, 14-15, 28-29; and knowledge of acquaintance, 14-15, 17, 28-29, 91, 117-118
Knowledge of acquaintance: definition of, 14-15; *See* Knowledge -about
Kordig, Carl R., 87
Kuhn, Thomas S., 87, 122
Language: and namelessness, 13-14; ordinary, 116-117, 120
Laws of nature, 27, 31
Lewis, C. I., 3
Life: as change, 36, 96; revaluation of, 105
Locke, 10, 55, 58, 117, 119
McDermott, John J., 4, 70, 118
Madden, Edward H., 110-111
Malleableness of nature, 23, 28
Mansel, Dean, 55
Mead, ix
Meaning of Truth, The, xi, 1-7, 38, 101
Mill, 71, 119
Miller, David L., 111, 117
Multiplicity of objects and relations, 10-11
Multiverse, 33
Namelessness, 13
Natural sciences: genesis of, 21
Neo-Kantians, 40
Nietzsche, 86, 118, 120, 122
Notebooks: James's, x, xiii
Novak, Michael, 116
Novelty, 64, 91
Objects: constitution of, 1, 10, 45, 53, 110-112, 118; of interest, 59, 62-63, 74
Objectivity, 16, 41, 95
Oliver, W. David, 116
Order: and chaos, 1, 30-37; as constituted, 48; created, 61, 64, 91
Ordinary experience, *See* Experience, ordinary
Pascal, 55
Passivity of mind, 18-27
Paulson, Friedrich, 55
Peirce, C. S., 2
Perception: passive or selective, 33

Perry, Ralph Barton, ix, xi, 7, 51, 54, 55, 89, 101, 118, 121
Perspective, 17-18, 23, 33-34, 86, 92-93, 95, 98-99, 106-108, 113
Phenomena of pure experience, 49, 51
Phenomenology, ix, 96, 118, 122
Physical and mental: criteria for, 42-45
Pillon, François, x
Plato, 75, 122
Pluralism, x, 2, 6, 35, 37, 77, 86, 100-101, 108
Pluralistic Universe, A, xi, 69, 83, 86, 89, 93, 98, 100-101, 120
Point of view, 2, 33-34, 95, 98, 113
Polanyi, Michael, 117
Pragmatic criterion, 28
Pragmatism, ix, xi, 3-4, 69-70, 74, 90, 102, 116, 119
Pragmatism, 111
Price, H. H., 67-68
Principles of Psychology, The, x, xii, 7, 10-32, 37, 39, 46, 52, 58-63, 66, 68, 88, 91, 93, 107, 115-116, 119-120
Process, 4-5, 90, 105; *See also* Transition
Projection, 32, 91
Pure experience, 3-6, 30, 34-53, 61, 64, 68-71, 82, 84-85, 90, 92, 96, 106-108, 111-113, 117-119; as hypothesis, 39-40, 44-46, 50-52, 71, 92-93; as neutral, 48-49, 51-53, 84, 92, 107, 112-113; as non-experiential, 49, 51-53; as paradigm, 48, 51-52; as perceptual immediacy, 48, 50-53; as metaphor, 92; plural formulation, 49-51; postulate of, xi, xii; status of, 51; *See also* Chaos, primal; Quasi-chaos; Transition
Quasi-chaos: of experiences, 46-48, 50, 85, 92-93; of pure experience, xii, 86, 107, 110; *See also* Tendencies
Quine, W. V., 110, 117
Radical empiricism, ix-xi, 1-5, 8, 29, 33, 38, 61-62, 68, 71-72, 74, 76, 89, 97, 99, 112, 116, 118; definition of, 1
Rationalism, 6, 32-33, 54, 71-72, 84
Rationalists, 10, 54, 75, 81, 99, 100, 117, 120
Realism, 24
Reid, Thomas, 55
Relations, xii-xiii, 12, 54, 107; and context, 6, 95, 101, 103; conjunctive, 5-6, 30, 61-62, 65-66, 70-77, 81, 85; constitution of, 1, 10, 84; directly experienced, x-xi, 1-2, 5-6, 12-13, 27-28, 31, 34, 38, 58, 60-70, 71-75, 83-85, 90, 99-106, 112; external and internal, 72-80, 99, 103, 120;

.